Instructions for using AR

LET AUGMENTED REALITY CHANGE HOW YOU READ A BOOK

With your smartphone, iPad or tablet you can use the
Hasmark AR app to invoke the augmented reality experience
to literally read outside the book.

1. Download the **Hasmark app** from the **Apple App Store** or **Google Play**

2. Open and select the ⟨⟩ option

3. Point your lens at the full image with the ⟨⟩ and enjoy the augmented reality experience.

Go ahead and try it right now with the cover image:

DARE
to Discover Your Purpose

ENDORSEMENTS

"Winston Churchill was just hitting his stride in his mid-sixties when he was elected Prime Minister of Great Britain and led the Allied Forces into WW2. Colonel Sanders, at the age of 65, began franchising KFC using his first Social Security check. *DARE to Discover Your Purpose* provides the mindset blueprint required to kickstart your so-called "retirement" years into high gear."

—Bob Proctor,
Bestselling Author of You Were Born Rich,
Toronto, Canada

"Jerjian's unique book can help retirees discover their life 'purpose.' His DARE method guides retiring boomers to delve into their hearts and minds to create a blueprint for a new life of purpose and passion in the third age of life. This book can help reframe retirement and transform obstacles into opportunities."

—Ken Dychtwald, PhD,
author of What Retirees Want and
Radical Curiosity, Orinda, CA, USA

"You can retire from work, but you can't retire from life. George Jerjian explains the vital importance of having purpose in later life and how to find it."

—Maggy Pigott, CBE,
Author of How to Age Joyfully:
Eight Steps to a Happier, Fuller Life, London, UK

"If you didn't tiptoe through most of your life, why would you 'tiptoe to a quiet death'? It's the fundamental question George Jerjian asks all of us to consider as he challenges us to re-evaluate what it means to live life with hope, optimism, and empowerment. We all should dare to live Jerjian's rebellious retirement."

—Peter Kaldes,
President & CEO, American Society on Aging,
San Francisco, CA, USA

"George Jerjian is a rebel with a cause. His cause is to awaken and inspire mid-lifers so they can prepare for the next stage of life. His key point is that every individual has the power to create a future that works for them, where they can flourish and prosper. But this will not just drop in your lap, it takes willingness and work. I commend George's work to you, so read this book, and get started on your journey of the rest of your life."

—Hunter Leonard,
Bestselling Author, Founder Silver & Wise, Sydney, Australia

"*DARE to Discover Your Purpose* is a life changing book for Boomers! By combining his graceful and easy to read writing style with his extensive knowledge, George Jerjian gifts seniors with the consummate "how to" book to craft a fulfilling retirement which most Boomers are inadequately prepared for, both financially and emotionally. For anyone who has a desire to live a joyful, and purposeful life during their remaining decades of life, DARE is a must read."

—Susan Stone,
Emotional Intelligence Instructor,
PSYCH-K Facilitator & Hypnotherapist Palm Beach, FL, USA

"George Jerjian's DARE method maps why and how to 'unretire' and provides the tools to help you find your own unique purpose."

—**Martin Hyde,**
Associate Professor of Gerontology,
Swansea University, UK

"*DARE to Discover Your Purpose,* sets out to rock the boat on our accepted ideas of retirement, reminding us that it is far more important to ask the question than it is to know the answer. George takes us on a journey of endless possibilities that awaits us in the Encore of our lives. The Hopi Indians say, "We are the ones we have been waiting for"."

—**Wallis Pattisonn,**
Founder of Bold not Old and Editor of
"Empowering Boldness" Melbourne, Australia

"With this timely book, George Jerjian fearlessly challenges conventional thinking on retirement and sets out his blueprint for a later life revolution."

—**Richard Murphy,**
retired Actuarial Partner at Lane, Clark & Peacock LLP
and currently Professor of Practice, University of
Southampton, UK

"To meet George Jerjian in person is one of life's great treats, but if you can't meet him personally, this little book of his will recharge the batteries of your life and change the way you think and behave. Wherever you go, you will create value and the planet will be a better place as a result."

—Professor Malcolm McDonald
MA(Oxon) MSc PhD DLitt DSc, Emeritus Professor,
Cranfield University School of Management, UK

DARE

To Discover Your Purpose

RETIRE • REFIRE • REWIRE

GEORGE JERJIAN

Editor: Harshita Sharma | harshita@hasmarkpublishing.com
Cover Design: Anne Karklins | anne@hasmarkpublishing.com
Book Design: Amit Dey | amit@hasmarkpublishing.com

ISBN 13: 978-1-77482-074-2
ISBN 10: 1774820749

CONTENTS

INTRODUCTION

What's my story?

What I want to share with you is a series of events that changed the course of my life in January 2007, when three unrelated events came together to create a perfect storm in my life. The first event was that we were moving homes, downsizing or right-sizing, if you will, and moving homes is a traumatic experience. The second event was that we received a phone call that my wife's father had had a stroke, so we had to drop everything and travel to Switzerland to see him. Within a week, he passed away and it opened a can of worms with the ensuing estate and legal matters. But it was the third event that was the most poignant for me. I had a hospital appointment for a colonoscopy, which proved successful, but the MRI revealed unwelcome news that a tumor, the size of a large eggplant, was sitting on my pelvis. An appointment with an oncologist at the medical center followed the next day and it was diagnosed that it was a bone tumor. The oncologist told me that in 98% of the cases, bone tumors are secondary cancer. This meant that it was too late to do anything as the cancer would have spread throughout my body. He gave me about six months to live. In the following three weeks, I underwent test after test, to confirm his diagnosis.

What surprised me was that I was not afraid of death. That startled me because I always thought I would be scared. But what was significant was that I'd look out the window across the river Thames, see the sun rising, and think, "How many of these beautiful sunrises will I see?" And what really troubled me was that my two daughters, who were teenagers at the time, wouldn't have their father with them as they embarked on their journey of life. After the three weeks of tests elapsed, I went to the oncologist, and he said that he had some good news and some bad news. The good news was that my bone tumor was benign and therefore I belonged to the 2% club. This meant I would survive! The bad news was that the bone tumor, which was large and aggressive, had to be removed by surgery, which implied some complicated cutting here and there. Ultimately, after two operations that went well, I had six months to recuperate on crutches and learn how to walk again properly.

This event changed the course of my life because it stopped me in my tracks. It compelled me to evaluate what was important and what was not. The way I saw it, and continue to see it, is that I am now living on "bonus" time. Each day is a gift. My life stopped in January 2007. Each day after that has been a gift. I cannot 'unknow' what I now know. So, I'm still on a learning journey. You'd think that God, the Universe, the Source, the Almighty, or whatever term you choose, would think that the cards dealt to me were harsh enough, when I was dealt a further harsh card.

My father-in-law's estate matters arose and I was asked to become involved. Since I was on crutches learning to walk again and recuperating at home, I thought this would be a nice way to occupy myself and do something useful. What I thought would take no more than 12 months ended up taking 12 years and more, and it's only now concluding. The case was about my father-in-law's business, which had gone into administration prior to his death because of cash flow problems. It was an asset-rich company, so I felt compelled to enter the fight to protect the interest of the shareholders, with whom I had reached an agreement to divide the spoils when we eventually won. In January 2016, nine years into the litigation, I was physically depleted and taking naps in the afternoon, which was unusual for me. My wife sent me to the doctor and blood tests were done, which revealed that my testosterone and my thyroid levels were at rock bottom of the ideal range. After examining and talking to me, my doctor concluded that it was the stress from the litigation that had caused it. He recommended that I settle the case if I wanted to live because medication would not be effective in this instance.

Unable to settle the case, I found another solution. I went away on a 30-day silent retreat near Snowdonia in North Wales, where all communication with the outside world was required to be severed. I had no access to the internet, to emails, to phones or mobiles. It was me, myself, and the practice of the spiritual exercises, conceived 500 years ago by a man known as St Ignatius of Loyola, founder of the Jesuit order. All the outside noise of the world was eliminated, and I was asked by my spiritual director, Sister Anne, to do an audit on my life. In my mind, I visited all the houses I'd lived in throughout my life and I searched for the crises and the opportunities in each home. I'm a writer, so I wrote everything down in my notebook. On meditating and reflecting on the stories that I wrote down, I discovered that none of the opportunities would've come about without the preceding crises. This was an awakening, an epiphany, and it resulted in my writing a book called *Spirit of Gratitude: Crises are Opportunities*, in which I focus on twelve crises and opportunities in my life that helped me. I've already shared one of them (my health concern) with you today to make my point. If you look back on your life and review your crises and your opportunities, you too will recognize that without the preceding crises, your opportunities wouldn't have revealed themselves. In the words of his song *Anthem*, Leonard Cohen sings,

"There's a crack, a crack in everything
That's how the light gets in."

Another crisis, another opportunity

The main reason I had gone to the silent retreat was because I was energetically drained from the litigation and could not go on as before. At this retreat, I found myself seeking and wanting to change the course of my life. I needed to find a new purpose, a new passion, that would give me a new North Star so that the litigation matter would become secondary in my life.

As I started to search for life coaches, I came across the usual suspects like Tony Robbins, but I had been to one of his gigs in London back in the late 1990s, and he did not resonate with me. One coach that did resonate with me was Bob Proctor, who was already in his 80s and still going strong. With me in my 60s, I was still young enough to have a guru who was older than me. Bob Proctor and I had one thing in common: a book that changed our lives irreversibly. That book was *Think and Grow Rich* by Napoleon Hill, first printed in 1937 and still in the top ten self-help books today. I read this book back in the 1990s and it changed my life. The single most important thing that I had taken away from that book was the word "persistence." It is that one word that has been my constant and consistent friend throughout my years in litigation. Without that book, my life would have been very different, and so much poorer.

A new leg of my new journey started in August 2017, when I attended a week-long live event with Bob Proctor in Toronto, Canada. It had taken me ten years after my bone tumor incident to reach this point. In that one week, I absorbed old and new material about how I could change my life. I felt revived, revitalized, and rejuvenated. In fact, I fell in love with this new mindset that banished fear and poverty of mind and invited in faith and abundance. I loved the material so much that I continued to work with Bob Proctor and his team for another 18 months.

At first, I started helping anyone and everyone. Eventually, I realized that it was not possible to help everyone, and I had to be selective. I was led to understand that the people I needed to help were people my age, people who were part of the baby boomer generation, those born between 1946 and 1964. In the process of understanding my clients, I came across one stumbling block, from which I had unwittingly escaped: retirement. I spent a great deal of time reading all I could about retirement—what it is, what it is not, its history, its promises, and its failures. After my near-death experience in 2007, I had been in a kind of semi-retirement for 10 years. Because I was focused on my litigation, I could do little else, apart from writing. I soon found myself bored, restless, and stuck. Semi-retirement had diminished my enthusiasm and energy and I'm certain it had also contributed to the big drop in my testosterone and thyroid levels. After my spiritual retreat, I had changed course and inadvertently "unretired."

With a view to serving my tribe of boomers, in mid-2018, I changed the direction of my new business. I created two things.

First, I created a company called "Retirement Rebellion," which is also a Facebook Group, because we all need "daring" and "energy" to emerge from the complacency of retirement. It's far too comfortable to stay where we are and to tiptoe to a quiet death (although that may take another 30 years for most of us, and we will most certainly outlive our savings). That is not what our life is about. Everything in life militates for energy because energy gives life. Retirement is a place to die, that's why it's sometimes been referred to as God's waiting room.

Second, I created a new 8-week program called "Dare to Discover Your Purpose," which I released in March 2019, after nine months of incubation, and just before the Covid-19 pandemic shut down the world. For the following two years, I've helped clients, written blogs, created podcasts, and filmed videos which I have shared on social media. Finally, I've written this book to share with you my journey and my transformation, out of retirement into a new life of purpose, passion, and prosperity.

Why carve out a new chapter in your life after retirement? Because retirement is a crisis, a turning point. In a sense, retirement is life knocking on your door alerting you to wake up to the fact that this is your last chance to implement your dream before the lights go out. For some of you, life is knocking on your door and shouting, "Wake up!" For others, life is whispering gently in your ear. Whichever it is, you ignore it at your peril.

Do not waste this crisis: grab the opportunity with both hands and discover what activity makes your heart sing and gives you a sense of purpose in life. I encourage you to start your journey reading this book with intention.

DISCOVER

ASSIMILATE

REWIRE

EXPAND

1

WHY RETIREMENT REBELLION?

"We cannot live the afternoon of life according to the program of life's morning; for what in the morning was true will in the evening become a lie."

—Dr. Carl Jung (1875–1961)
Swiss Psychiatrist and Psychologist

Wh19at Carl Jung was saying in essence is that in the morning of life, we are trained to seek achievement, accolades, and ambition, much like the chlorophyll in leaves and plants seeks to absorb the sunlight to get its nutrients and energy. In the evening of life, not only does it take too much energy to seek achievement, accolades, and ambition, but it also provides us with too little satisfaction. After retirement, we need to seek new challenges to grow; we need to seek purpose, passion, and prosperity. Much like the leaves in the fall, which return to their true colors. In other words, we can't use the attributes that we exercised in the morning of life and extend it to the evening; life changes and we need to change with it. This is the start of our journey in this book.

Why is a Retirement Rebellion necessary?

The first point is that the average life expectancy has risen to 83 years in the US and UK, and it is expected to reach 100 in the near future. This factor alone has effectively broken the retirement equation.

The second point is that by adding another 20 to 30 years to retirement, it has made it almost longer than our working life and as a result, almost all of us will outlive our savings. It is mathematically an impossibility to save for that length of retirement, without sacrificing a significant portion of our present. In his book *What Retirees Want*, Gerontologist Ken Dychtwald writes that "the average cost of retirement is now over $1,000,000 and that the average 60-year-old pre-retiree has saved only $135,000…This is a recipe for mass elder poverty."

The third point is that retirement is essentially sleepwalking to a quiet death. In fact, everything we've been told about retirement is a myth. It's a life of illusion and mirages. I'm here to bust that myth so that you can think of your life as a life of purpose, and the way I'm going to do it is to ask you to dare to discover your purpose in life. Why dare? Well, because you're a rebel and because you need courage to emerge from the complacency of retirement or to "unretire."

So, what are we to do?

Let's start with the definition of retirement. The Merriam-Webster Dictionary defines retirement as a withdrawal from life, withdrawal from active life. And that's the operative word—withdrawal. Nothing in nature withdraws; it is either growing or dying. So, withdrawing from life is essentially surrendering to death and that is what traditional retirement is about, so the very definition is wrong when it comes to retirement. It is an industrial age concept that we have absorbed, and because we've been programmed, we don't dare to question or challenge it.

People confuse pension planning with retirement planning. These are two different concepts. If you Google search the words "Retirement Planning", all you will see, for pages and pages, are savings-and pension-related sites—that's all you get. There is nothing on actual retirement planning, which is about your life, and not about money. Now don't get me wrong, money is important. Your pension monies are important, but what's more important is your life planning. What is it you're going to do with the rest of your life? You can retire from your work, but you can't retire from life, and it's crucial to understand the difference.

Retirement is a crisis in the true sense of the word; it's a turning point. All transitions in life are generally celebrated, and retirement is no exception. Yet in the last 10 to 20 years, a vast majority of people have been retiring partially. So, commemorating and celebrating this important transition has lost significance because most retired people are compelled to find new work to supplement their income. In other words, they have one foot in the world of retirement and the other foot in the world of work. This inconsistency is like living in two minds, and it has an impact on our overall health and happiness. For many, this stage of retirement is not clear cut, and this is important to acknowledge because retirement has gone the way of dial-up broadband; we have a whole new way of living and retirement has no place in our state of living.

So how did we get here? The way we got here is because we've all been programmed. Our parents were programmed by their parents, and their parents before them. And it just cascades down time, but to try to understand what retirement is about, we need to take a step back into history.

What is the History of Retirement?

a.   The Origin of Retirement

Well clearly it originated before the Romans, but it was the Romans who really took it to a new level. When the young Octavian ascended to power and took the name of Caesar Augustus, he was following in the footsteps of his uncle Julius Caesar, who was stabbed in the Senate some 15 years earlier. Clearly, the assassination of his uncle must have affected the young Caesar Augustus, who was not a warrior like Julius Caesar. He was a highly intelligent young man and he understood that he needed the Imperial Roman army on his side, so what did he do? He created an entity called the *Aerarium Militare,* which was, in essence, a pension fund for the Imperial Roman army, and he put in six million sesterces of his own family's money. This is confirmed by the historian Suetonius, who wrote that Augustus did this to secure the loyalty of the Imperial Roman army.

The Roman army pension was extraordinary at its time. A Roman soldier would receive a pension of a cash lump sum, followed by twelve years of pay, paid out over time, and some of the senior soldiers also received land. Granted, the land was invariably on the periphery of the empire where land was cheaper and more dangerous, but pensioned officers would have locals tilling the land for them and paying them a percentage of the proceeds. Of course, there were conditions. A Roman soldier had to serve for about 25 years and be involved in about 16 military campaigns, but this was a good pension fund and Caesar Augustus' *Aerarium Militare* became a huge investment pot. So much so that it did not last beyond the lives of the next two emperors, because the Roman senate borrowed against it, and ultimately depleted it.

In the United States, pensions started to be paid around the 1860s to municipal workers, policemen, and so on, particularly in New York City. But it did not really kick off until the military started receiving the offer of pensions, which President Lincoln introduced to recruit soldiers during the US Civil War (1861–65). After the Civil War, the US government continued to pay a pension to the veterans to ensure that veterans did not resort to pillaging the general population and creating civil unrest. In 1875, the American Express Company introduced the first personal pension plan and that was the beginning of the commercial use of pensions across the board. About 20 years later, in the 1890s, the railway companies, which were making a great deal of money, wanted to retain their workforce so they introduced a pension for their employees. It's worth mentioning that the railway companies in those days were what the internet companies are today—they were drivers of the booming economy.

In Europe in 1883, Otto von Bismarck, the Chancellor of Germany, was worried about the Marxists and their seductive message to the German people, so to pull them away from Marxism, he introduced pensions. Being very conscious about their security, the Germans bought into the pensions story, hook, line, and sinker. Bismarck was no fool. He had set the retirement age at 65 years when life expectancy for the average German was 58 years (a seven-year difference), so the fact that most Germans would never have made it to the age of 65 made it feasible and workable. Bismarck's plan worked like a dream and ultimately, 65 became the magical retirement age across the world for more than a century.

Back in the United States, during the great depression in the 1930s, a Californian by the name of Francis Townsend introduced this idea that the government should pay every American $200 per month as a pension for those who were retiring. We need to remember that $200 a month was the sort of average going rate. This horrified the US President Franklin Delano Roosevelt, so he decided that he had to do something. So, in 1935, Roosevelt introduced the Social Security Act with one major difference: the government wasn't going to pay anyone; people had to pay into this pension fund.

b. What is the Recent History of Retirement?

In the 1990s, Mary-Lou Weisman, a *New York Times* writer, wrote an article about how retirement started exploding in the 1910s for the wealthy. They slowly started moving to Florida, and there they started creating communities of retirees where they had plenty of leisure. Leisure became sort of an aspiring thing to do. The only problem was that the wealthy retired people didn't want to see the people who were working anywhere near them—they didn't want to feel guilty. And this was the beginning of the retirement frenzy, which resulted in golf courses mushrooming across the state of Florida. From 1921–1930, the number of golf courses tripled in Florida. On the back of this, the leisure industry started to grow, and of course, over time, you had the entertainment industry that was built to supplement this—the cruise liners, the travel industry, Hollywood movies, and now Netflix and so on.

So, why do so many wealthy people not retire? What's interesting is when you ask ordinary people why wealthy people continue to work, it astonishes them. They cannot understand why wealthy people continue working when they have so much money. So, why do wealthy people not stop working? What ordinary people don't understand is that wealthy people take all the vacations they want, but being on a permanent vacation doesn't satisfy them. After two weeks, they're bored. They want something that gives them purpose, that excites them, and makes them want to jump out of bed. Sitting by a pool sipping Martinis all day doesn't do it for them. The secret is that wealthy people continue working because they love what they do, so it's not work for them. The ordinary person who is ready to stop working, does so because they do not love what they do. The wealthy person might stop doing the work that created their wealth, but they recreate a new life for themselves and give themselves a new purpose. That's why wealthy people don't retire. In fact, they hate retiring. And it's not just wealthy people, it's the people who have had successful careers. Take the examples of singer Dolly Parton, actresses Dame Maggie Smith and Dame Judi Dench. None of them retired; they'd rather be taken out horizontal. Look at Warren Buffet, Bill Gates, and Sir Richard Branson. They recreated their lives. They continue doing something new that inspires them, and we should take heed from them because if they, who have all the wealth in the world, still continue working, they're doing something right – not something wrong. So, the secret is to work at something you love to do. Forget the money; that comes afterwards.

There is another issue here that we need to cover in terms of how we got here, in terms of the outside world—looking at events and things that have changed in our world today. I call them "tectonic shifts," and the first one is how corporations have plundered pensions.

Award-winning *Wall Street Journal* journalist, Ellen Schultz, wrote a book called *Retirement Heist*, in which she gives endless examples of companies that have plundered their employees' pension funds. One such company, GE (General Electric), had $25 billion in its pension fund in 1999. Twenty years later, they have a debt of $6 billion. This is a huge loss. Think back to Caesar Augustus's pension fund for the Imperial Roman military, which was also depleted by loans taken out by the Roman Senate. The sad fact is that when you have a rich nest egg like that, people just can't take their eyes off it. And that's what happened with the Fortune 500 companies who faced financial difficulties after the year 2000. In collaboration with the management consultants and benefits consultants, these corporations devised new strategies as to how they could exploit their pension funds for the benefit and survival of the company. Their plausible argument was why should their corporation, providing employment to hundreds of thousands, make significant cuts, or for some even collapse, when they had access to loans from an affiliated healthy pension fund.

So, these Fortune 500 companies were encouraged to borrow against their own company's pension plans. For example, a company like GE would have had hundreds of subsidiaries, whose pension funds would have been segregated, and when sold, would have gone with them, making it so complicated and impossible to untangle. In a sense, it was a similar (but less toxic) exercise as what caused the 2008 financial meltdown: a significantly large financial instrument called CDO (Collateralized Debt Obligation), where mortgage bundles were sliced and diced in such a complex manner that they were impossible to untangle, and so became unsalable and worthless. As to the pension funds of the Fortune 500, according to Ellen Schultz in her book, they became so diluted that for many of the Fortune 500 companies, they went into debt.

c.   The Politics of Retirement

In the late 1980s, both the US government and the UK government recognized that more of their people were living longer and that pensions were being paid out for a longer period of time, and this was becoming a huge drain on their finances. Longevity was creating a massive problem in financing guaranteed pensions. So, they decided to change the goal posts. Over time, they planned to move away from "guaranteed benefits" pension schemes to what was called "guaranteed contributions." Guaranteed benefits guaranteed a pension at retirement of a large percentage of current earnings of employees. Guaranteed contributions means only the contribution that you make into the pension is guaranteed, not what pension you receive at retirement. So, in one stroke, pensions were diluted, and the guarantees vanished. The outcry was short-lived, because the pain would not be felt by the vast majority of the population for many decades.

In the UK, what happened next was that the tax benefits were also slowly taken away. Under the Conservative government, Chancellor Norman Lamont chipped away at the ACT, a tax benefit, and then under the Labor government, Chancellor

Gordon Brown eliminated it altogether. The elimination of this tax benefit translated into what was then a £5 billion chip at the pension funds. Nobody felt anything at the time. Why? Because it didn't touch anyone's pocket immediately. This was something that was going to happen in the future, so it slipped away from the popular mind.

In the US, the value of unfunded obligations in 2020 has increased to over $50 trillion; these are monies that do not exist as such. US economist Paul Krugman says that we have a looming crisis in retirement. With 10,000 baby boomers (our tribe) sleepwalking each day into retirement, we could be looking at mass elder poverty, unless we act now.

Another point which changes the whole dynamic of retirement is that we have a New World Order emerging and the Old Order is dying. The New World Order that's emerging is really our move into the internet and online, and the way that everything is connected. It's changing the way we work, the way we do business, and the way we live, and yet, our economies and politics have not moved in alignment, so this is another issue of tectonic shift. The Old Order is dying but the new one is not strong enough and has not delineated its economic and political power yet—so we are in this place of interregnum, between the two.

This is something that's causing confusion and, as we've seen, has resulted in Brexit and the election of Trump changing the dynamics around the UK, the US, and around the world. You will have noticed that we have more authoritarian regimes. People want more security so they're leaning to the past. They want more security so they're demanding it in the ballot box.

The pandemic that started towards the end of 2019 has accelerated this dynamic. Where do we go from here? Well, I don't have the answers on the world outside us, or how to control it.

However, I do have answers on how we can take command of our own lives, because that is the only control we have.

d.   The Future of Retirement

The retirement equation is broken. Longer life expectancy has created a situation where retirees will receive less pension money because we are living longer and there is less money in the pot. Also, the population of our planet is almost 8 billion people and growing, but what's also happening is that the older people are growing as a percentage of the population. The UN statistics show us that by 2030, in Europe (including the UK), the population over the age of 60 is going to increase to 35%. One in three people are going to be over the age of 60, and we're getting to the point where the senior people are going to outnumber new births. This is significant. In North America, the number is slightly better at 28%, but it's still going in the same direction.

One of the most underserved sectors of the population is the elderly, or the "boomers." They are retiring in droves, and I repeat, about 10,000 people retire each day in the US alone. None of these people are prepared for retirement. Yes, they may be partially prepared financially, but most retirees sleepwalk into retirement. They are oblivious to the challenges that await them. With the stigma of ageism, finding work becomes difficult and eventually people give up and stay home. People no longer see the "retired" because they are not seen as useful units in the society. Retirees become invisible; they become ghosts. Even the advertising world is not interested in selling to them. Yet this seasoned cohort of people already form almost one-third of the population and spend 60 cents out of every $1 spent in the economy. What a terrible waste of human and financial

resources and paradoxically what an amazing human and economic opportunity!

What's my point, you ask? My point is this: Boomers need a
rebellion to change their own mindsets about retirement before
they can change anyone else's. Ageism is not outside us: it is
within each of us. One significant reason why retirees are ghosts
is because we've lost faith in ourselves. We don't disagree with
the zeitgeist of our era that "youth" is beautiful and should be
worshipped, and "old" is ugly and should be discarded. If we
don't disagree radically with this theory, then are we not ageist
ourselves? Are we not hypocrites when we rage about ageism,
when we are ageists ourselves? Time to take a stand. We need to
create a new dynamic, a new economy of boomers, by boomers,
and for boomers. To achieve this, we will require a rebellion so
that boomers can take charge of their own lives.

Professors Lynda Gratton and Andrew Scott, in their book,
The 100-Year Life: Living and Working in an Age of Longevity, explain
how the old traditional three-stage life is gone. Stage one is the
education part. Stage two is the working life, and stage three is
retirement after 65. That model is gone. Gratton and Scott offer
a new model called the Multi-Stage Life where, when you come
to retirement, you're not really retiring. Instead, you're creating a
new opportunity to start the next stage in your life, where you
could be working until the age of 90. The only difference is that
you should be working at what you really enjoy doing, as that's
the only thing that's going to sustain you in the long run.

I resonate with their suggestion because it's so obvious and
yet we don't recognize it. They draw a red line at this three-
stage life, with the age of 65 as retirement age, because with a
further 20 to 30 years more of life expectancy, mathematically,
there is no amount of money you can save for that stage of

life without further work and savings. Even if you were to save half your money through your entire life to provide for the last 30% of your life, the sacrifice required would make no sense. What's more, even with all the sacrifice, it would still be a big risk because you don't know your date of death.

So, what Gratton and Scott suggest are numerous examples of how people can transform their working lives at 65 or before. But without one essential ingredient, any transition would be difficult. That ingredient is a change in your mindset. When you reach the age of 65, it is no longer a terminal date. It is the start of a new life.

★   ★   ★

2

THE REALITY OF RETIREMENT

"Iron rusts from disuse; water loses its purity from stagnation… even so does inaction sap the vigor of the mind."

—Leonardo da Vinci (1452–1519)
Florentine polymath, inventor, sculptor, painter, drawer

Let's consider what the Florentine polymath Leonardo da Vinci described about inactivity. They didn't have retirement in his day, but he understood the general idea and the consequences of not being productive in one's life. Now, Leonardo da Vinci understood human anatomy because he did enough work on it, and he understood about the mind, and he realized that when we don't use our minds, we become weaker. So, we need to be active and energetic in the physical world that we live in.

What do I know about retirement?

Well, I have no intention of retiring. If you recall my story in the introduction, I experienced a perfect storm in my life in 2007 and I ultimately ended up funding a litigation of my father-in-law's estate. Instead of one year, it took 12 years and more, and it's only now coming to an end. But in that same period, I was, for all intents and purposes, semi-retired because I couldn't do anything else as I had to keep my eye on the ball. But litigation was only taking an hour or two of my day, so what was I doing with the rest of my time?

I was filling time. I'm a writer, so I wrote a novel for three years. The story was loosely based on my litigation, and writing it felt therapeutic to me. The working title was *Less is More*, but I couldn't publish it because it was to do with the litigation I was involved in, and even changing names and places would not protect me from being sued. The point is that I was filling time writing books. I was also acting as a consultant in a commercial real estate venture in the US. So, in essence, I had a portfolio of work, but I wasn't getting a buzz. I was simply filling time and it was sapping my energy. In 2016, after the ninth year in litigation, I found myself exhausted in the afternoons and taking one-hour naps. My wife urged me to see our doctor, who, on seeing my blood test results, discovered that my thyroid and testosterone levels were extremely low, which was why I was feeling so weak. The doctor told me that no medication would help for long, because my condition was clearly linked to the tension and stress caused by the litigation. Unable to resolve the litigation without losing everything, I had to seek another solution, which led me to my 30-day silent retreat. The point I am making is that clearly, my life needed another crisis for me to wake up.

In a nutshell, I did experience what it was like to be semi-retired, and I hated it. I don't ever want to go back to those days; there was no joy in it whatsoever. Yes, I had free time, but I was filling it with unnecessary activities just to keep busy—there was no thrill. As humans, we need to be engaged, socially as well as mentally.

What is your single biggest challenge in retirement?

Retirement means different things to different people. If you ask people what retirement means to them, you will get a different response each time. I did a deep dive survey of individuals over the age of 60, and I asked them this one question: "What is your single biggest challenge in retirement?" To give you a flavor, I have listed a small selection of responses I received, word for word, and categorized under the following headings—health, money, purpose, and identity:

Health

Keeping my mind and body young and healthy.

Fear of dying in pain and discomfort.
When you're 70 with a heart condition, you don't get that many more bites at the apple.

Money

Money going out, nothing coming in.
Fear of poverty and losing dignity.
My husband lost a significant amount of our retirement money.

Purpose

My greatest fear is stopping work—work that I love.
I retired from my teaching position, but I am not retired.
I will never retire; I enjoy doing what I'm doing.

Identity

Fear of losing my identity created over a lifetime.
People do not see you anymore.
Feelings of rejection, internalized, not voiced.

I also offered a quiz on my website in 2020 and 2021 and I asked the same question, "What is your single biggest challenge in retirement?" Over 23,000 people completed the entire quiz and specifically this question. The results are shown in a pie chart below. 50% of the people selected "health" as their single biggest challenge, 35% selected "finance," and 15% selected "lack of purpose." What you will discover reading this book is that the single most important thing after retiring is having "purpose." If you have "purpose" after you retire from your work, your health and financial concerns will, for most of us, evaporate.

My online Quiz Question:
"What's Your Single Biggest Challenge in Retirement?"

23,000+ quiz participants as at 30 June 2021

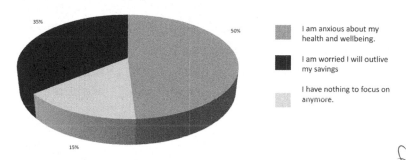

	I am anxious about my health and wellbeing.
	I am worried I will outlive my savings
	I have nothing to focus on anymore.

Retirement is an unnatural habitat.

I've already explained we're either growing or dying. Aimlessness is a vice, which leads to catastrophe. It is a timeless message that we should stay away from it.

A study was released in November 2019 by the IZA Institute of Labor Economics in China alongside Binghamton University of the United States, which revealed that over the past 10 years, they had been monitoring retired Chinese individuals who had been receiving pension from the state. The most significant discovery in this study was that this group of retired individuals showed cognitive impairment because they were not working. They were just aimless, and they were not focused on doing anything specific. As a result, they experienced impairment to their cognitive abilities, which leads to dementia and Alzheimer's. We know that our aging populations in the UK and in the US are also experiencing the very same outcome. So, if we do not use our mind, we can be certain of losing it.

The Nobel Prize-winning economist Edmund Phelps said that "working is essential to the good life." If you love what you do, you won't have to work another day. So, if you don't love what you do, then you're in the wrong business and retirement is not going to solve the problem for you. You shouldn't wait until retirement to do something you love to do, because retirement is not the remedy for unhappiness. You must choose to make that decision: decide to do something you like to do. No one can make this decision for you. No doubt, those in your past, whose permission you might have sought, are long gone. The decision is yours, and yours alone.

To simplify the reality of retirement, I have broken it down to three segments. First, energy sustains our lives; second, the skyrocketing impacts on our health; and third, the shame of retirement.

a. Energy Sustains Our Lives

For centuries, spiritual sages have said that we are spiritual beings having a physical experience, rather than physical beings having a spiritual experience. The difference is immense, and science has come on board with that understanding, starting with Albert Einstein who famously said, "Energy cannot be created or destroyed; it can only be changed from one form to another." By this, he meant that our spirit, our energy, doesn't die with us. We don't know where it goes, but it must go somewhere. So, let's take this idea one stage further. If we are energetic beings, we need to be in the flow, and when we're not in the flow, we're not in our energy. If we are not in the flow, then we must be stuck. If we are stuck, it means we are not growing, and if we are not growing, then we are dying. On his deathbed, Leonardo da Vinci, with long flowing hair and beard, was visited by the king of France, and his last words were reputedly, "There's so much to do and so little time." Taking the example of Da Vinci, we need to be in the flow until our last breath.

DaVinci has been an inspiration to many people. For example, one of my mentors, Bob Proctor, who is a success coach in North America, has been coaching for over fifty years. He's now in his mid-80s and is still going strong. He does not stop, and he won't stop until his last breath.

Another person who inspires me is Professor Malcolm McDonald—the UK's oldest marketing guru. He's also in his mid-80s. He was my professor of marketing at the University of Bradford Management Centre back in the 1970s. I saw him in 2019, and he was still traveling the world, giving lectures, and being welcomed by universities around the world. He's even starting a new video course. He doesn't stop because he loves what he does—it's what gives him joy.

b.   The Skyrocketing Impacts on Our Health

BBC Online Health Editor, Caroline Parkinson, wrote that 3 out of 5 cancers occur in individuals over the age of 65. That means 60% of cancers occur in people over the age of 65. Perhaps not such a surprising number, but significant nonetheless.

What are the leading causes of death in the United States?

For more than 30 years, the Centers for Disease Control and Prevention (CDC) have been collecting and examining causes of death in the United States. In 2017, the top 10 causes of death in the United States account for more than 75% of all deaths. The top two account for almost 50%.

In the illustration below, which focuses on the European Union, the major causes of death of people age 65 and over are shown compared to the major cause of death of those of all other ages, and the contrast is alarmingly clear.

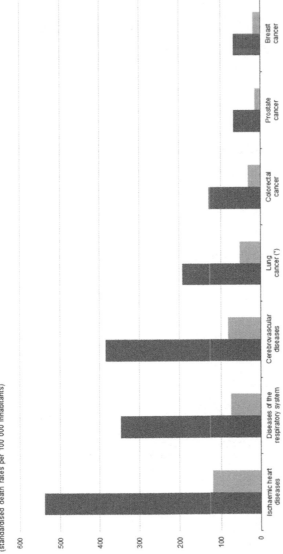

Major causes of death, EU-27, 2016
(standardised death rates per 100 000 inhabitants)

■ Persons aged 65 years and over   ▬ All persons

Note: the three most common causes of death among persons aged 65 years and over are diseases of the circulatory system, cancer and diseases of the respiratory system.
(¹) Trachea, bronchus and lung.
Source: Eurostat (online data code: hlth_cd_asdr2)

eurostat

It would be an incomplete discussion not to include deaths from the Covid-19 pandemic. The illustration on the next page, released by the CDC in October 2020, shows very clearly that while Covid-19 "cases" were spread across all age groups, 95% of the "deaths" occurred in the age groups from 50 to 85 and above.

Another health aspect is inactivity, which, in retirement, increases over time. Inactivity means that we're depleting our energy. Our energy is like a battery—if we don't use it, we start to lose it. So, we must strive to be active, but active with spirit (because we *want* to be active, not because we must).

The illustration on the next page shows the prevalence of various chronic diseases and disabilities among men and women aged 50–74 years of age in the US, England, and Europe. What is compelling is the prevalence of mobility impairment ranging

The 95 Percent

Coronavirus cases and deaths by age group

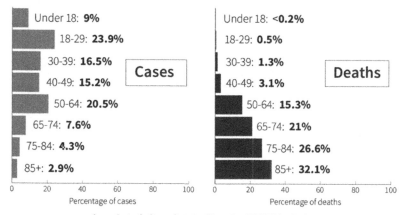

Source: Centers for Disease Control and Prevention, CDC COVID Data Tracker.
Based on available data as of Oct. 29, 2020.

AARP

from 45% in Europe to 60% in the US and hypertension ranging from 30% in Europe to 45% in the US.

Another aspect that impacts our health is loneliness, because human beings are social animals. From the minute we're born, we need the milk of human connection and when that connection is broken, we are left alone, our social needs unsatisfied. Solitude is a positive aspect of being alone and is invariably one of the choices. Loneliness is a negative aspect of being alone and, invariably, is not a choice. Being "alone and lonely" is a most painful emotion that gnaws at the human spirit. Loneliness, which is rampant in retirement, also leads to mental health issues.

A 2021 study[1] of 12,825 adults over the age of 51 published in the Journal of Applied Gerontology provides new evidence that:

1. Strong purpose in life has been associated with healthier lifestyle behaviors.

2. Strong purpose in life has also been associated with slower rates of progression of chronic illnesses.

3. Above average purpose in life and life satisfaction may serve as a proxy for increased resilience and continued social participation.

c.   The Shame of Retirement

The final point I want to make is about the shame involved in retirement. This is something that most people don't talk about: it's the unspoken word. Professor Teresa Amabile of Harvard

---

[1] Multimorbidity and Social Participation is Moderated by Purpose in Life and Life Satisfaction, by Jamie E. Luster, David Ratz, and Melissa Y. Wei - https://doi.org/10.1177%2F07334648211027691

Figure 8.
Prevalence of Chronic Disease and Disability among Men and Women Aged 50-74 Years in the United States, England, and Europe: 2004

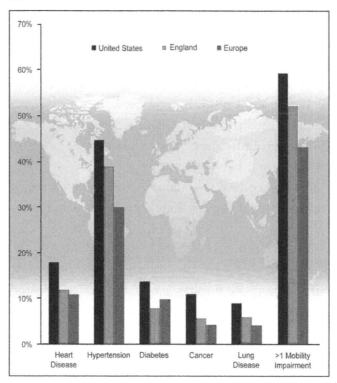

Source: Adapted from Avendano M, Glymour MM, Banks J, Mackenbach JP. Health disadvantage in US adults aged 50 to 74 years: A comparison of the health of rich and poor Americans with that of Europeans. *American Journal of Public Health 2009*; 99/3:540-548, using data from the Health and Retirement Study, the English Longitudinal Study of Ageing, and the Survey of Health, Ageing and Retirement in Europe. Please see original source for additional information.

Business School did an extensive study on retirement and how people feel and what they say in retirement. Her claim to fame is the idea of what she calls "Identity Bridging."

What does that mean? I'll give you an example. You meet someone at a party and you ask them what they do. They tell you they are a "retired lawyer," or a "retired librarian," or a "retired janitor." The truth is that they're no longer a lawyer, a librarian, or a janitor: they are simply "retired." So, why do they not just say that they are retired? Professor Amabile states that it is because they believe being retired makes them into useless nobodies, ghosts, and so they bridge their current identity to the persona they were before retirement to give themselves a semblance of self-esteem.

But the expert on the topic of "shame" is none other than Professor Brené Brown, author of the book *Daring Greatly*, and professor at the University of Texas in Houston. The extensive research that she has done has been mostly on women and (latterly) on men. To give you a snapshot, her research findings are that women seek perfection and to please. They seek perfection in how they look, perfection as a wife, perfection as a mother, perfection as a daughter, and so on. And with men, (no surprise here) it's about strength and power. So, whether it's on the sports field or in business, it's always about strength and power. And in a sense, when we reach retirement, we men have to take off our armor and, when we take off our armor, we become vulnerable. We become vulnerable in the sense that we can easily be wounded.

Retirement is a new stage in our life. What we fail to see and understand is that there's power in vulnerability, once we accept ourselves for who we really are. Just look at children, or adolescents, when they're thinking about maneuvering in the world. They start to lie a little bit and we realize they're actually pretty bad liars because they can't lie very well. As they grow up, they become more polished at lying. They become more polished at maneuvering in the world, and the polished lies become like a second skin. But when we reach retirement, and our armor and identity is taken off, we feel naked and ashamed. We ask ourselves, who are we now? At this point, a salient question to ask ourselves is: How does shame impact on us?

Professor Brown compares shame to having termites in a house. Like termites, shame starts in the dark, behind the walls of retirement, if you like. Slowly, it chips away at the wood structure. Before we know it, the staircase of our self-esteem has collapsed, and not long after, everything crumbles. So, beware that retirement comes with a huge health warning at all levels—health, identity, and financial.

We will outlive our savings

Pensions, savings, and investments are very crucial, but they are not the central point of my argument. Our focus, and that of the financial services industry, has always been about money. On the internet, the overwhelming information on "retirement planning" is focused majorly on the financial aspect. But "retirement planning" is not just about money and savings. In our world today, it's even less about money, because just focusing on money and savings is like rearranging the deck chairs on the Titanic. You need to go to the main cause of why the retirement formula is broken.

The reason it doesn't work is because retirement has been fixed at the age of 65, and retiring baby boomers are likely to live up to the age of 90 (possibly 100). So, if we retire in our 60s, we've still got 25–30 years to go. How are we going to fund this retirement? We're always going to have this question as a

'Sword of Damocles' hanging above our heads. We're going to be constantly worried about scarcity—about not having enough money to take us through the rest of our lives. So, there's a lot of unspoken worries that we carry with us, and the more time we have available, the more time we have to worry. My point is that we need to reverse this mentality completely. We need to overturn this way of thinking. At the moment, money is on the top and planning is on the bottom. We need to reverse it, so the planning is on top. This alone changes the dynamic.

If we're going to last an additional 30 years, then clearly retirement is (mathematically) not an option. We need to be engaged and living, not just so that the money lasts, but so that we continue living, because if we stop working and living, we are going to slowly die. Harvard Business School Professor Rosabeth Moss Kanter said that the age of retirement is over. She essentially said that baby boomers would create a new stage in life. She has understood this for many years now and what I'm saying is, we need to understand how we can engage this period of retirement to create a new stage in our lives. In the ancient past, old people were considered wise and were revered. In our consumer society, everything is expendable, including old people. As rebel baby boomers, it is our duty to challenge this toxic thinking, just as we have challenged every other part of our lives. We must make this change, not just for ourselves, but for future generations. We have an obligation to ourselves to live our lives to the fullest.

If I haven't been clear, let me make it perfectly clear. For 99% of us in our 60s, retirement is no longer an option because we're not going to have enough money to sustain us comfortably in our old age. If in our 60s, we know we have another 30 or even 40 years to go, the whole idea of retirement should be ditched. Now your pension and investments are safe on one side, but if you continue working at what you love to do and being productive, you will get paid and you won't have to worry about money, savings, and investments. In fact, you'll be so busy enjoying what you're working at that worry doesn't even come into the equation.

Since the 1980s, a vast number of retirees have retired partially, because they could not afford to retire fully. This creates a different problem. Where there's no clear delineation between the end of work and the start of retirement, there is no turning point: there is only a twilight zone. So instead of being stuck in the twilight zone, as hundreds of millions of retired baby boomers are, I encourage you to find your North Star, to dare to discover your purpose, to discover who you are meant to be.

Irish playwright George Bernard Shaw said, "Men don't quit because they get old, they get old because they quit." So don't quit. Start your new life. You deserve it, and you can do it.

★   ★   ★

DISCOVER

ASSIMILATE

REWIRE

EXPAND

3

THE MINDSET REBEL

"Thinking is the hardest work there is, which is probably the reason so few engage in it."

—Henry Ford (1863–1947)
Founder, Ford Motor Company

Thinking is the hardest thing to do in the world, that's why so few people do it. These were the views of Henry Ford, the founder of Ford Motor Company. There is no consensus as to how "thinking" is adequately defined or understood, yet what we do know is that the process of "thinking" is indeed hard. After his first automobile, the Model T, debuted in 1908, Henry Ford is reputed to have said, "If I had asked people what they wanted, they would have said faster horses." In other words, traditional (logical) thinking alone would have produced "faster horses," yet it took a different kind of thinking, the hardest type of thinking, to produce the automobile.

If we want to think smarter, we must understand how our minds work. Until several years ago, I thought I knew what thinking was, but in retrospect, I didn't. Thinking isn't just about using our brains in the traditional sense of the word. It is not just a process of mental activity where the flow of ideas can lead to a logical conclusion. For our mind to leap into action, our mind needs to think in pictures, and when we don't have pictures in our mind of what we are trying to achieve, then our mind cannot process what we desire. To be clear, our brain is not our mind.

Differences between our brain and our mind

When I ask you to picture your car in your mind, you'll be able to picture it. You know what color your car is, you know what make and model it is, and you can picture the interior in full color. If I ask you to describe your cell phone, you can picture the make and model, what it looks like, and you can describe your favorite apps and everything that it can do for you. But if I were to ask you to picture your mind, you would struggle. If I were to ask you where your mind is, you would most likely point to your head, because that's where your brain is. But your brain is not your mind. The brain is simply an electrical switching station. That's all it is. So where is your mind? Your mind resides in every cell of your body, all 50 trillion of them. For example, have you ever experienced a situation where your mind and your body were in flow, in sync, and in alignment? Did you feel a sense of effortless flow? That's because both your mind (conscious) and your body (subconscious) were aligned.

Over the past centuries, our education has focused exclusively on the conscious mind, and very little on the subconscious. The Jesuits, a Catholic religious order founded in the 1540s, focused their Christian mission on "education," and what they discovered was that if they could educate children up to the age of seven with their moral compass, they knew that should those children (now adults) stray from their course, they would always return. The Jesuits understood the power of the subconscious mind. They knew that the subconscious mind, once imprinted, works like a thermostat, where the temperature rises and falls, but always within a set range.

Our two minds: conscious and subconscious

Just as our brain consists of two hemispheres, left and right, our minds also consist of two distinct parts: the conscious and the subconscious.

Our conscious mind

Our conscious mind is our thinking mind, and the conscious mind represents about one percent of our entire mind. The conscious mind has access to all our basic senses—seeing, hearing, smelling, touching, and tasting, and much more. The conscious mind also has access to certain intellectual faculties such as perception, will, reason, imagination, memory, and intuition.

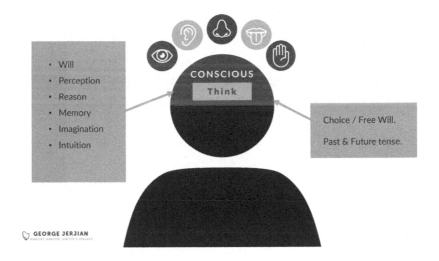

Our perception is our point of view. When we see something that causes us to think that it can't be done, we can change our perception of the situation and create an idea of how it can be done.

Our will gives us the ability to hold one picture on the screen of our mind to the exclusion of everything else. This gives us the ability to laser focus and concentrate, and with practice, our will can be strengthened.

Our reasoning is what gives us the ability to think. Thinking is our highest function. It is our inductive reasoning that gives us the ability to have original thoughts and bring them together to form ideas.

Our imagination creates fantasies, which is the first stage of creation. Retirement Rebellion was a fantasy when conceived in my mind. Everything is created twice: once in the mind, and second, when manifested in our material world.

Our memory is perfect. There is no such thing as a bad memory. There are only strong memories and weak memories, and they simply need exercise to strengthen them.

Lastly, our intuition picks up vibrations in our minds. It permits us to know, and to know that we know what is happening around us. I believe that intuition is derived from our "feeling" mind, not our "thinking" mind. It is only when we stop the noise in our thinking mind that we can then allow ourselves to intuit. It is about "listening" with our entire bodies, not just our ears. It is a higher faculty that can be developed to an extraordinary degree.

Let's take a deeper look at memory. For most of us, memory is almost invariably associated with our past memories. Over our lifetime, we've had billions of experiences, but the only ones we remember are the ones to which emotion is attached. For example, if you were bullied at school and the experience was painful, you will remember that incident because a feeling of pain is attached to that event. If you had a joyful experience with your first lover, then you will remember that too. Without what I call the "emotional molecule" attached to a specific memory, we wouldn't remember it. It's because of the emotional impact it had in our lives that our mind retains it. But what we haven't considered is using memory for future events that we want to happen in our lives and attaching an emotion to it, so as to embed or fuse that to our memory. This is something that can be done.

In today's popular culture, people call this process "manifestation." The reason manifestation works is because we have imagined a future memory that we desire and then attached an emotion to it. We need to appreciate the difference between the conscious and subconscious minds when it comes to the concept of "time." You see, the conscious mind can only think in the past and in the future, whereas the subconscious mind thinks only in the present. For example, have you ever driven to a destination that took several hours, and when you arrived at your destination, you could not recall that you had driven there? That's because your conscious mind was preoccupied (about the past or the future), whereas your subconscious mind, which lives in the present moment, took control of your car and drove you to where you had wanted it to go.

Our subconscious mind

The subconscious mind is the "emotional" mind. The subconscious controls everything that our body does—sleeping, digesting, walking, driving, and so much more. Everything in our subconscious has been programmed from everything that we've learned from childhood onwards. These subconscious programs are crucial for us to live the wonderful and magical lives that we lead. Without these subconscious programs, we would have to learn everything anew each day. Imagine waking up in the morning and having to learn how to walk all over again! Imagine having to learn how to eat again. How tedious would life be?

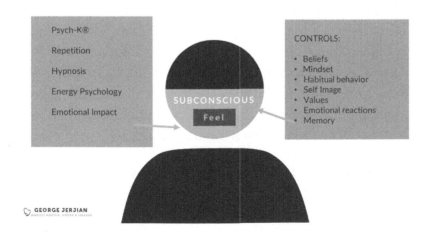

That said, we also have programs that are no longer working for us; they're obsolete. In fact, worse than obsolete, they sabotage us, and these are the ones that we need to eliminate. So how can we eliminate them? We cannot eliminate them, but we can record over them, as it were. We can do so by replacing them with new ones. Now, the subconscious mind is the "emotional" mind, the "feeling" mind, and it is very powerful, and we must harness the emotional mind to any idea or belief that we want to have. Why? Because without the engagement of our emotions and feelings, no progress can be made. The emotional mind is always in the present moment. Just think of pain—if our body experiences pain, everything is focused on that pain. It needn't be, but our body is hollering, and we will listen. That's being in the present moment. Thinking in the present moment—that's what the subconscious mind does.

The subconscious mind is also the repository of our beliefs, our paradigms, and our self-image, so whatever self-image we have, that is what will show. Whatever inner dialogue we have in the back of our mind, that is what will be expressed in our body and in our thinking, so we need to be very careful and aware of what our mind is thinking. Our conscious mind may be thinking of changing something in our lives, but if our subconscious mind is not in agreement, then that change will not happen.

Later in this chapter, we will look at how to change our subconscious mind. In the meantime, there is another element to thinking that is profoundly important but often ignored, and that is the awareness that sits behind our thinking.

Awareness: We Are Not Our Thoughts

The concept of thinking is neither straightforward, nor is it linear. A person can hold two contradictory thoughts, which are equally valid, in their mind. For example, here is one thought: When we retire at, say, the age of 65, we baby boomers are likely to live up to the age of 90 and beyond. This thought is true. Another thought is that no one knows their date of death, so in theory, it is possible that some of us may not live past this evening. This thought is also true, even if an unpleasant one. Our mind does not like uncertainty, so it will generally choose to ignore the second thought. A realistic or proper way of thinking requires us to be able to hold two contradictory thoughts which are equally valid in our mind. If we choose to avoid doing so, then we are deluding ourselves of a possibility that is true and real.

There's a new aspect of thinking that I'd like you to consider or become aware of, and that is that we are not our mind. We are separate from our mind. What do I mean when I say, "We are not our mind"?

What I mean is that people generally think that whatever they're thinking originates within them, but our thoughts are separate from us. Who we are and what we are thinking are two separate things. Thoughts come and go; they're not ours. Imagine you are a lighthouse on a rock, looking out on a bay, and your thoughts are the ships that sail across the bay. Every time you have a thought, it's a ship that sails across the bay. You decide whether that thought is what you want or not. However, what we tend to do is grab the thought, emotionalize it, and say, "This is mine." It is not. They're just thoughts. So, if we are not our thoughts, who are we then? Well, we are the awareness behind that thought. Just ponder on that.

You are the awareness behind the thought.

Imagine you're sitting on a bench in a garden. Stop thinking. Become aware of your breathing. Take a deep breath in, hold it and count to six, then slowly release it. If a thought comes into your mind, dismiss it immediately, and don't berate yourself. Let it go. Return to your breathing for another two sessions. It's difficult to stop thoughts from coming in, but you get the idea that you are aware of your inner self, and that thoughts are separate from you. You are not the thought (whatever the thought might be). It's not you. You are that breath, that awareness behind that thought. Now why is this important to understand? It's important because it shows you there is a difference between your awareness (who you are) and what you're thinking (your thoughts). If there is a difference between who you are and your thoughts, it means you have the power to control your thoughts. If you're thinking negatively, it's because you've emotionally chosen to engage with that negative thought. All you need to do is release it; it's not yours. You can choose positive thoughts and get positive results.

Here's another example. You have a thought that a particular person is horrible, and then an hour later, this same person does something nice for you unexpectedly, and you change your mind. "That's such a sweet thing to do; they're so nice." Now imagine these two contradictory thoughts expressed to you by a stranger. What would you think of this person? You'd think they were a hypocrite for expressing two contradictory thoughts. You wouldn't be able to trust somebody like that, would you? And yet, we trust ourselves with contradictory thoughts, so you can see why these thoughts are not us. They are outside us, yet we're the ones who grab these thoughts and take ownership of them. Next time you struggle with a "fixated" thought, just think of the monstrous character, Gollum, in *Lord of the Rings*, and his lust for his "precious" ring.

To help you understand visually, here's a picture of the faces of thinking as follows: you have your conscious mind upfront, your self-awareness immediately behind it, and the subconscious mind behind that.

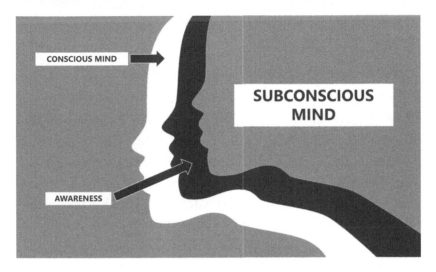

95% of the time we are sleepwalking

In his book, *Breaking the Habit of Being Yourself: How to Lose Your Mind and Create a New One*, Dr. Joe Dispenza talks about how we're programmed to do what we do each day. 95% of the time, we're making decisions based on programs which have, for the most part, been created by other people (our parents, society, education, our culture, and our friends). We are programmed, and what we need to be aware of is that some of these programs are now toxic and they sabotage us from doing what we want to do. We must make sure that we engage with those programs that are sabotaging us and turn them around. This is particularly true in retirement, where these programs are fused in, and difficult to remove. I want to assure you they're not as difficult as you think. If you've got the will and the desire, you can change them.

Consider this. If 95% of the time, our subconscious mind is programmed, this implies that 95% of the time we're sleepwalking through our lives. Now that you're in retirement, and time is of the essence, ask yourself this question: do you want to sleepwalk to a quiet death, or do you want to go out with a bang?

How can we change our subconscious mind?

There are certain ways to change the subconscious mind. While the conscious mind seeks stimulation to function, the subconscious mind seeks repetition. When we make our New Year's resolutions, we believe we can bring this about simply by using our willpower. So, why is it that for the great majority, our New Year's resolution lies in tatters within a few weeks? The reason is that our subconscious mind sabotages it because our resolution lies outside the thermostatic range of our subconscious program. So how do we change our subconscious mind? We can access our subconscious mind to change whatever it is we want to change, and it can be done by repetition.

For example, we may have an affirmation that we repetitively say to ourselves daily for a number of months, and presto, it will happen. This is a long and time-tested way of doing it, and it works. Another way is hypnosis, which is not only very effective, but also faster. Yet another method is Psych-K, which integrates our left brain and our right brain hemispheres so that we respond in a whole brain manner, and it is also the fastest. More on this in Chapter 5.

If we want to change our results, we need to change our thinking. So, for example, if you're retired, and you believe that you're too old to find work, that no business will hire you, and that's why you can't find work, then that is exactly what will manifest in your life. If you have these negative thoughts swirling in your mind, this negative inner dialogue churning inside your head, this thinking is going to produce negative feelings for you. These negative feelings will create negative actions, and these negative actions will give you the results you've manifested— which is that you can't find work.

Conversely, if you were to change your thoughts to something like, "I am an energetic person, I provide value, and I have transferable skills" and you engage only these thoughts, and you seek where you could use these, that creates a feeling that you want, which is, "I am worthy and I deserve good things to happen to me." Those feelings will create the positive action you desire, invariably because the subconscious mind is the domain of feelings, and feelings result in actions, and these actions will create the results you want. Once you have those good results, they will reinforce the good thinking and so create a virtuous cycle. What are you waiting for?

★   ★   ★

4

THE REBEL MIND

"Energy cannot be created or destroyed, it can only be changed from one form to another."

—Albert Einstein (1879–1955)
Mathematician and physicist

I hear you say, "I'm too old to change." If you think that you're too old to change, then that is true for you and that will be your outcome. If you think you can change and you have a desire to change, then that too is true and that will be your outcome. As energetic beings, we're all capable of change and transformation. It was an eye-opener for me to discover that I was not the personality I thought I was. Our personalities are not written in stone. Each of us developed our personalities from a childhood experience, positive or negative, that had a deep impact on our minds and from which our perspective on the world was formed.

To understand what makes a rebel mind, we need to have a deeper understanding of who we are or perhaps take a helicopter view. A good place to start is with Greek philosopher Plato, who wrote that our lives on earth are bookended by death. What Plato meant was that before we were born, we were non-existent on the physical plane, then we are born and exist on the physical plane, and then we die and once again, we are non-existent on the physical plane. In other words, in the language we can better understand today, we are spiritual beings having a physical experience, not physical beings having a spiritual experience.

In his book, *The Biology of Belief: Unleashing the Power of Consciousness, Matter & Miracles*, cell biologist Dr. Bruce Lipton shares this wonderful analogy to describe who we are in a more scientific way. He suggests that we look at an old 1960s television set—remember those? The television set sat inside a large wooden box that featured as a furniture piece in homes at the time. Let's assume you were watching the program "Bonanza" or "Perry Mason" or "The Invisible Man" when suddenly, the television broke down completely. Did that mean that the program was dead? Clearly not. The program could be viewed again if you purchased a new television. Once connected, you could watch your program again. So, what is the analogy of the television set and our human existence? Well, the television is our physical body, and the transmission of the program is our spiritual energy. Just because our physical bodies die, it doesn't mean that it's the end of our spiritual existence. Our transmission, our spiritual energy, remains alive. We are, after all, energy, and as Albert Einstein said, "Energy cannot be created or destroyed." As spiritual beings, or energetic beings, energy flows through us. What's natural comes through naturally.

We're taught from an early age to control ourselves and to control things. We're taught that this is not just for our benefit, but also for the benefit of our families, our tribes, and our nation. Now, I have no argument with discipline, which is essential to lead a good life. However, like everything else in life, excess discipline is bad for us and can lead to blockages of energy. The truth is that most of our illnesses are energy blocks because we're trying to control things. Our conscious mind is blocking our subconscious mind. This clash between our thinking mind and our emotional mind creates a roadblock. We generally try to maneuver around these roadblocks, which only provides us with temporary relief. To let things flow naturally, we need to remove the roadblock altogether.

Why is this important? Because in retirement, we need to let go of the things we're trying to control, such as our finances, our budgets, and even our spouses. That's what makes us ill. By letting go of the control, we're letting go of our fears of what the outcome might be. We think that by controlling the outcome, we're secure. We do not achieve security; we're simply making things worse. So, in retirement we need to let the energy flow.

Consider this. What is it you love to do? What is it you want to do? Let yourself express it. Remove the fear blocks. Remove the energy blocks. The energy blocks might be something like, "Well, if I do what I want to do, my spouse might leave me," or "If I do what I want to do, I might lose a good portion of my pension savings."

Whatever it might be, there's always something that you're doing for somebody else, but remember that you are priority number one. If you're unhappy, how can your spouse or your family be happy? First, seek what makes you happy, and everything else flows from there.

Is everything we see "real"?

This is not a trick question. We generally think that we are defined by our personalities. We think they are rock solid. Nobel Prize-winning physicist, Niels Bohr, said that everything we see as real, cannot be regarded as real. The word "real" means "thing" or "matter." But matter does not just have a physical existence; it also has an energetic existence, through its atomic and sub-atomic particles. Bohr challenged us to see "matter" through the lens of energy.

His quote, "No, no, you're not thinking; you're just being logical," captures the spirit of his argument.

What is Bohr talking about? What he's talking about is that our worldview is Newtonian, as in Newtonian physics, where everything is logical and linear, A to B to C to D, whereas we live in a natural world, a quantum world, as in Quantum physics, where everything is holistic and organic. When we move from the linear world thinking to a quantum world thinking, how we see our world changes, and how we think changes.

Is everything we see real? Clearly, what our eyes see is not the whole picture. Not everything is visible. Reality is nuanced because much is hidden in nature, and much is kept secret. So instead of stating that "things" and "matter" are real or physical, it would be more correct to state that "things" and "matter" are, in fact, energy, whether their atoms are light (as in air), or dense (as in wood or stone). Remember, Einstein said that energy cannot be created nor can it be destroyed. Also remember the television analogy, where we saw that even when the television broke down, the transmission remained, because energy cannot be destroyed. It's the same with us. Humans are not just physical beings; we are also made of energy. We are energetic beings, where every molecule within us is energy.

For example, abandonment is a wound. If, as a child, you felt abandoned, you couldn't rationalize it, but your actions and everything you've done since that incident is seen through your lens of that abandonment, and your drive or purpose is to recover from that position of abandonment. When you experienced abandonment in your childhood, your psyche created an emotional wiring and firing of the neurons and synapses in your mind, so you look at the whole world through that perspective of abandonment, and hence your personality developed with that skew. But your personality need not be static for the rest of your life, because it can be modified. In fact, this is the perfect time to change because it will open a whole new world of possibilities for you, which you cannot see from where you stand now.

Why are we addicted to our emotions?

Much of our "thinking" is, in fact, embedded in our emotions, in our subconscious mind. 95% of our thinking is done by our subconscious programs, so it shouldn't be a surprise that we make decisions based on our emotions and then justify them with reasons.

In his book, *Breaking the Habit of Being Yourself: How to Lose Your Mind and Create a New One*, Dr. Joe Dispenza shares how we are addicted to being who we are. That is so because every time we have a thought, that thought releases neurochemicals into our mind and instructs the body to do whatever it has to do. If we have a good thought, we're releasing certain neurochemicals that are good for us, and if we have bad thoughts, we're releasing neurochemicals that are toxic for us. Imagine when we think badly of someone. We are not harming them, we are harming ourselves. Therefore, when we think well of people and wish them well, even if we think they don't deserve it, we're doing ourselves a favor. After all, we are all on a journey in this life. Yes, it's easier said than done, but it's the right way to think.

Addictions impact our lives at all levels. Some people who are ill are reluctant to get better because they are fearful that they will lose the attention they are currently receiving. Can you see how problems become addictions and people are reluctant to let them go? It's the same in retirement. We're too comfortable and complacent in our aimlessness in retirement, and even when we know it's damaging us, we're reluctant to change. We know change requires we make an effort and we simply can't be bothered. What are you addicted to? When you try to pull away from your addictions, you will encounter strong resistance. That's why you need energy to emerge from this situation. Hence my call to rebel against the status quo, because the status quo is slowly killing you.

Let's go back to our personality. Over our lifetime, we have developed a certain personality and a certain number of emotional responses. In neuroscience, this is explained by Hebb's law, which states that "neurons that fire together, wire together." Because these neurons and synapses that are firing and wiring in our minds create a chemical reaction in our bodies, we become addicted to these chemical reactions, and we even get high on them.

When we are in a situation that makes us feel vulnerable and threatened, our subconscious mind takes over. Neurons and synapses are triggered, and we become fearful or angry, and we react. Our conscious mind shuts down. We're now in flight or fight mode. We are prisoners of our thoughts and feelings. If we're constantly reminding ourselves of past experiences, as a filter for every incident we experience from this point on, all we're doing is falling back into the old experiences or paradigms.

Think of a road rage experience you may have had. You're tired, you're stressed, you've been in the car for hours, and you're almost home, when suddenly a car from a side road cuts in front of you. You are livid. You cannot believe the audacity of this idiot. You press on your car horn for two full minutes. A narrative starts to develop in your mind, which triggers your neurons and synapses to wire and fire, releasing chemicals into your body. You are now getting a high. This is toxic for you, and what's worse is it will have no effect whatsoever on that driver in front of you. So, who are you punishing?

As memories are the bedrock of this addiction, we need to change the memory, story, or beliefs we tell ourselves. If we don't do so, we're going to get the same results. So how can we change our memory, story, or belief? How can we get new experiences, so it opens a whole new world for us?

Reverting to the road rage example above, what if you change the story you tell yourself? Why allow toxic emotions to overwhelm you when you can choose a healthy response, allowing you to be gentle with yourself. When that car cut in front of you, you could say to yourself that this person needs to cut in front of me because he desperately needs to go to the hospital because his daughter has been in an accident. Empathy ensues not just for that person, but for yourself. You've now fired a new set of neurons that will wire together and release good chemicals into your body that will deliver a very good outcome. What's more, our subconscious mind cannot tell the difference between reality and fiction, so why does it matter that this story may be fiction? We cannot control what other people think of us no matter how hard we try, but we do have control over what we choose to think.

In neuroscience, the negative side of Hebb's law states that "neurons that fire apart, wire apart." Effectively, this means that if you do not use it, you'll lose it. It's a bit like a spider's web. The spider throws out a filament and continues to throw out a filament repeatedly until that filament becomes firm and strong, and the old ones slowly wither away from lack of use. It's the same with our neurons and, in fact, these neurons that fire and wire together also create our personalities. They're the signatures of our personalities. If you influence your brain to experience a new event before it has happened, it creates the neural networks for it to happen. If you keep installing, reinforcing, and reengaging these new neural networks, this creates the pathway for a new software program for your mind.

How do we install a new software program in our minds?

What a strange notion to compare our minds and cells to a computer. What's even stranger is that our cells behave just like a computer chip, declares Dr. Bruce Lipton, who has done extensive work on cells. What Dr. Lipton discovered about the cell, which is crucial when we talk about reprogramming our mind, is that the purpose of the nucleus is ultimately only for reproduction. In other words, the nuclei are effectively the gonads of the cell, and not the intellect. That is not what we were taught in biology when I was at school. How far we have come.

What Dr. Lipton discovered is that the membrane is the brain, and the membrane is what connects the cell to all the other 50 trillion cells in our body. While these 50 trillion cells live wrapped in our bodies, these cells are not prisoners in our body. When we interact and engage with other humans, so do our cells. This fact is embedded even in our language. When we say, "I have chemistry with somebody," it is our cells that are engaging. Yet, what is most remarkable about Dr. Lipton's discovery is that "each cell membrane is a liquid semiconductor, with gates and channels, which means that a cell is, in effect, a programmable chip."

The fact that cells are programmable is a huge discovery. It also confirms the belief that we can change our personalities and gives credence to the idea that we are beings of energy. Now why is this important when we reach retirement? It's important because when we retire in the traditional sense, we've made the decision not to be in active work, and so we've elected to disintegrate and die. We choose to deliberately slow down, which is an unnatural state, because our bodies need energy and activity to remain healthy. To better understand this, consider the fact that our outer intestines have tens of billions of cells that need replenishing every 72 hours, and to do that, we have to be energetic and active. We must be engaged mentally, physically, and emotionally to stay healthy.

So, on the basis that slowing down and retiring prevents our cells from replenishing and growing means that traditional retirement is bad for our health. In nature, as in life, we're either growing or dying. For example, if your body is attacked by an illness, it goes into what is termed "protection mode," and all the systems shut down to protect everything in that area of hurt. This is a temporary situation, and when things get better, the body returns to growth. In contrast, retirement is not a temporary situation, but a permanent one. What happens in retirement is that everything starts to shut down, because you're saving resources, you're saving money, and you're not operating fully in growth mode, so everything starts to become smaller and shrivel. Is it possible to be in "protection mode" and "growth mode" at the same time? In principle, it is possible, but it is very inefficient and damaging, because it's like driving with one foot on the accelerator and the other foot on the brake.

Let's look at another example of protection and growth modes: savings and investments. You have a choice—do you want to invest for "capital growth," in which case you invest in stocks and shares, or do you want to invest for "protection of capital," which means investing in cash and bonds. In theory, being in cash and bonds will protect your assets, but there will be no growth, and therefore your assets will depreciate over time because of inflation. Whereas, if you've invested in stocks and shares, you're in "growth mode," and you might lose some of it because stocks and shares are volatile assets, and their values go up and down. This is the only way that our bodies, and our savings, can continue to grow, and in retirement, we're not talking about our final years here, as we may still have another 20 or 30 years to go. We still need to be in "growth mode." We need to be in an optimistic state of mind.

The Rebel Mind needs "visualization" or envisioning. We need to have an image of a worthy vision that we desire, and that worthy goal becomes our one and only North Star. So how does this work?

Well, let's look at the animal world. Have you ever seen a cat try to jump over a wall? The cat will look to the top of the wall, look down at the base, look up to the top of the wall again, and look down at the base again. It will do this a dozen times, maybe more. Then, when it finally makes that move to jump, it has already seen itself at the top of the wall. You see the same story with basketball players. The control, the visualization, and then the ball is through the basket. We must set ourselves a vision, then emotionalize it by adding emotional molecules to that new future memory, and then imagine we've already achieved it. We must build the neural pathways in our mind, so the path is set. The rest is just a follow through. We believe that we've already arrived before we have arrived. That's what makes it happen.

Have you ever experienced a moment where your conscious mind and subconscious mind were so aligned that whatever activity you were involved in was seamless and effortless? That's what a Rebel Mind does. Ask yourself this question: What possibilities are you missing out on because your mind is blocked by old programs that sabotage you?

We have this notion that we live in a universe. We don't live in a universe; we live in a multiverse. Which universe are you living in now and what multiverses are available for you to benefit from if you only had the opportunity to see it, to visualize it? Once your mind has expanded, it cannot go back to its original size. So, I dare you to craft and create a new life, full of passion, purpose, and potential, that will allow you to glide through the next 20 to 30 years.

★   ★   ★

DISCOVER

ASSIMILATE

REWIRE

EXPAND

5

CREATE YOUR REBEL MINDSET

"The subconscious mind is like a tape player. Until you change the tape, it will not change."

—Dr. Bruce H. Lipton (1944–)
Developmental Biologist, and author of
The Biology of Belief: Unleashing the Power of Consciousness, Matter & Miracles

Fear and faith are abstract notions—whatever we believe in, that will be our reality. From our early childhood, we have been instructed in what to believe in and what to fear. Our culture, religion, tribe, extended families, and parents have seen to that. That's why the subconscious mind is like a tape player or a tape recorder, if you will, on which our beliefs and stories have been recorded by others, and not by us. In later life, when the landscape of our world changes, and the map in our minds no longer matches the reality on the ground, we are compelled to change the way we think. If we wish to survive and thrive, we must revisit, review, and reform what we believe in, and if what we believe in no longer serves us, we must then change the stories we tell ourselves. If we want our subconscious mind to change, then we must record a new story over the old tape or change the tape altogether.

Spiritual Dimension

Before we investigate how we can change our subconscious mind, I want to touch on who we think we are as individuals. Clearly, as I've mentioned before, we are physical beings, but we're not just physical beings—we're so much more. In a sense, we're spiritual beings having a physical experience, and this isn't just a religious notion.

German-born physicist Albert Einstein's theory of special relativity expresses the fact that mass and energy are the same physical entity and can be changed into each other. In the equation, $E=mc^2$, the increased relativistic mass (m) of a body times the speed of light squared (c^2) is equal to the kinetic energy (E) of that body. Einstein understood the connection between physical matter (m) and kinetic energy (E). Matter and energy are deeply connected, just as our bodies and spirits are.

Einstein didn't start the equation with "mass" (m), the physical side. He started with the kinetic energy (E) side because we, as beings, are energetic. So, I want to touch on what the ancient masters taught about energy and spirit. One example is the Sufi mystic and poet, Rumi, who wrote extensively and beautifully about the connection of spirit and matter, and who we are as individuals. He captured this wonderful analogy that if God was the ocean, we as human beings are drops in the ocean. He went on to qualify that it would be a mistake to say that we are just drops in the ocean, because we are so much more than that. We are "the ocean in a drop." When we are drops in the ocean, we are insignificant and worthless. Conversely, when we become the ocean in a drop, it changes the entire dynamic of who we are. Just as a drop has the ocean in it, we also have God within us, and thereby assume divine powers. We are transformed from what is powerless to what is powerful. We're not as limited as we think we are. We have limitless power within us. How can we use that power if we do not believe it exists? We must first believe in its existence, so that we can use it.

Another example is Jesus Christ. He talked about how powerful we are, and he said that we were sons and daughters of God as He was. Some might think this is blasphemy, but how is that possible when these are his own words? It gets even more insightful in the next statement, "...Whoever believes in me will perform the same works as I have been doing and they will perform even greater works" (John 14:12). Now, this is extraordinary when you think about it. How could we possibly do "even greater works" than He did? Did He not raise people from the dead? Did He not perform miracles? Yet, He's saying to us that we can do that and even more? Is it we who are limiting ourselves? In my mind, the answer is yes, we are. We limit ourselves because that's how we've been programmed.

A final example is Marianne Williamson, prolific author and Christian spiritualist, who reveals that "our deepest fear is not that we're inadequate. Our deepest fear is that we're powerful beyond measure." Nelson Mandela used her words at his inauguration as President of South Africa because it was a speech of empowerment. We are much more powerful than we think. In fact, we're not afraid of our darkness; we're afraid of our light. We're afraid of how powerful we are, because if we accept that we're that powerful, it means we're at risk of losing the approval of the people we love and care about—our families, our friends, and our tribe. We fear losing them if we become that powerful. We fear that they will withdraw from us, so we squirm back into the darkness.

To change our results, we need to change our thinking.

Mental Dimension

We spoke about this in previous chapters, but I'd just like to extend this a little bit. If we want to change the results, we must change our thoughts first. Our thoughts then impact on our feelings, our feelings impact on our actions, and our actions impact on our thoughts, and so the virtual circuit is completed. So, what are the three attributes that are important to recognize in this thinking process that we're trying to change?

The first attribute is "persistence." Napoleon Hill, one of the first self-help authors and author of the best-selling *Think and Grow Rich*, interviewed over 500 men of fortune and accomplishment in the United States in the early 1900s and he found that this was the one exceptional attribute that they all shared. He went on to qualify it: "*Persistence is to the character of man as carbon is to steel.*" It's their backbone.

And persistence is one characteristic that successful people have. They can have all the other attributes, but if they do not have persistence, they will not succeed. So, persistence is a prerequisite to success. Whatever you embark on changing in your life, you must persist until you win. And you will be tested. You will want to give in, but you can't, and you mustn't.

The second attribute is "attitude." Attitude was described by James Allen, the English philosopher, as the one thing that changed everything in his life. *"The greatest discovery of my generation is that a human being can alter his life by altering his attitudes."* This is as true today as it was then, and will be true forever.

The third attribute is "self-image." Self-image is something that only recently has come into our consciousness. The inner dialogue that you have in your mind is crucial to your own well-being. Dr. Maxwell Maltz, a plastic surgeon in New York City in the 1970s, undertook many operations to change people's faces and bodies to make them look better and improve their aesthetics. But what he discovered in his surgeries was that post-surgery, half of his patients liked the result of what they saw after the operation, and it improved their lives and the way they thought about themselves. Yet, for the other half of his patients, nothing changed. The inner dialogue they had prior to the operation remained unchanged. They continued to see themselves as ugly or not good-looking. This pushed Dr. Maltz to further research this matter.

He managed to discover that inner dialogue is the most important thing there is in changing your self-image. Inner dialogue is even more important than plastic surgery (although the latter continues to do very well). But it's not plastic surgery that changes things, it's the inner dialogue that you have with yourself. So, if you think you're ugly, then you will feel ugly, and you will believe you're ugly. Alternatively, if you think you're beautiful, and you feel beautiful, then you are beautiful. Whatever you believe is correct. Fear and faith are abstract notions – whatever you believe in, will be your reality. It's always our choice.

Emotional Dimension

Emotion is a very powerful tool. The mind is both the "thinking mind" and the "emotional mind." In the West, we dismiss emotion, and we don't give it sufficient credit. We disdain and distrust it because people can manipulate us and use emotion to press our buttons, so to speak. And so, we distance ourselves from emotions, but in doing so, we cheat ourselves, because emotion is part of our thinking, and part of our being. The Danish physicist Niels Bohr captured it in one sentence: "No, no, you're not thinking; you're just being logical."

Contrary to what we have been taught, the intuitive mind (the emotional mind, or the feeling mind) forms the more important part of our thinking. Albert Einstein understood this when he said, "The intuitive mind is a sacred gift and the rational mind is a faithful servant. We have created a society that honors the servant and has forgotten the gift."

Thinking requires the integration of our thinking (conscious) mind and our emotional (subconscious) mind. Our mind is not in our brain. Our mind is in every cell of our bodies, all 50 trillion of them. Yes, it's true that thought is the most powerful thing in the world—but thought must be harnessed to emotion to generate power. Without emotion harnessed to it, thought is just hot air. Our educational system has, for centuries, focused on the conscious mind, which represents about 1% of our minds, and it has completely ignored our subconscious mind, which represents 99% of our mind. This is such a waste of human capital. We need to recognize that we can no longer ignore the power of the subconscious mind. If we want to truly activate our minds, we need to engage our thinking mind with our emotional mind. The way to do it is to take a thought and emotionalize it, desire it, or as I like to say, attach an emotional molecule to it. Neville Goddard, author of *Feeling is the Secret*, wrote, "The subconscious mind will accept our thoughts only if they are fortified with our feelings." If an idea is to impact our lives, it must be harnessed to our emotions, without which it cannot take flight.

Now let me explain this. Consider all your treasured memories of your past, of your youth. The only reason you're able to recall them is because there was an emotional molecule attached to those memories. You have millions of memories of activities you've experienced throughout your life which you cannot possibly remember (thankfully, for most of us), but those that you do remember are instances that impacted emotionally on you. Whether good or bad, you remember them because there's an emotional molecule attached to them. Whether it's a birth, a marriage, a divorce, loss of your job, treachery, betrayal and so on. Whatever it is, a good or bad memory, as soon as you have an emotion attached to it, your subconscious (emotional) mind will retain it.

How can we change our subconscious mind?

When we talk about creating your Rebel mindset, we're talking about envisioning a new reality for yourself. This is something that comes out of your imagination. Your imagination can create a new reality, a new future memory, if you will.

Here are three questions for you to consider deeply:

1. What is it that you really want?
2. What is it that you're afraid of?
3. What activity do you enjoy, in which you lose all sense of time?

Don't rush these. Write them down and carry them with you wherever you go and scribble down your thoughts.

Get as clear as you can about what you wish to manifest and write it down somewhere so that you're constantly aware of it. Writing it down not only helps you clarify exactly what you want, but it also sharpens the setting of your intention. Now go deeper into your vision. What do you see? What do you hear? What do you feel? It's most helpful if you use all your senses, especially your visual, auditory, and kinesthetic senses, because that is what the subconscious mind requires to take you to where you want to be. So, collect images and put them on your vision board or in your alchemy box, so that every time you see the images, it brings up the feelings of love, joy, and fulfillment that are important in amplifying your manifestation. Manifestation requires you to set a goal using your conscious (logical) mind and then using your subconscious (emotional) mind to step into imagining that you are already living it. Both parts of the mind must be engaged. That heightened state of being is already within you.

Once done, you must engage with this manifestation several times each day, using all your senses, and try and retain that feeling of success and achievement. Keep cultivating a complete sense of knowing that you are already living your desired life, each morning as you rise, during the day, and certainly at night just before you sleep. Remember that the subconscious cannot differentiate between what is real and what is fantasy, and so it is very powerful to imagine that you have already achieved your desired goal. The adage "fake it till you make it" is not a myth or a fantasy. It is, in fact, true, and it works like a dream. It works because you are building new neural networks in your brain to mirror your desired result. Your heightened emotions trigger your neurons to fire and wire together to bring this about, much like a spider that throws out filament after filament to build its web.

One last suggestion: Be grateful that you have already received your heart's desire, and this attitude of gratitude will give you the altitude you desire. More on this in Chapter 7.

Once you have created this "new reality," you need to emotionalize it. You need to attach an emotional molecule to that future memory. You need to bring it into the present moment because that's where the subconscious resides. When you emotionalize it, you retain it in your memory. Your subconscious mind records it, and will play it back repeatedly, with your assistance. This is the power of emotion. Remember, we said the conscious mind only thinks in the past and in the future, and the subconscious can only think in the present moment. The "now" is the only thing that exists for the subconscious mind. Don't forget that your subconscious mind is managing your entire body, without you being aware of it: your sleep, your digestion, your body, when you drive a car, and so on. Everything you do—sitting down, getting up, picking up a glass of water, drinking it, putting it down—every action you take in any given hour is run by your subconscious programs. Your subconscious mind is operating in the present moment, allowing your thinking mind, your conscious mind, to think about the past and the future.

If you focus on the past, you cannot move forward. Memories of the past keep us tied to the past. The past is gone and will never come back. You can never step into the same river again because it is not the same water. If you are to move forward, you must let go of the past. Make peace with your past, and then move forward with a new dream. Your mental programming is all based on your memories of the past. You need to create a new memory, a future memory, through visualizing, through envisioning. Then you add what your five senses reveal to you to bring it into the present moment, and then you attach an emotional molecule. This must have "meaning" for you; you must feel it. That's how your subconscious mind will retain it.

So how do you bring this new vision to life?

Our subconscious mind cannot tell the difference between what is real and what is fantasy. Whatever you plant in it, positive or negative, that's what you'll reap. The subconscious also requires knowing exactly what it is that you wish. If you're in two minds about it, which literally means your conscious mind and subconscious mind are not aligned, then nothing will happen.

To bring it to life, to make it real so your subconscious mind recognizes it as real, you need to share with it what your senses will see, hear, and feel when you have achieved your goal. So, let's look at it on the visual, the auditory, and the kinesthetic levels.

a.   Visual

How will your subconscious mind know that you've achieved your goal? How would you know? What will you see?

What I suggest to people is to think in terms of what will be seen on a video. How would you video the event of you achieving your goal, as it's happening, in real time? Avoid using abstract words or thoughts. The subconscious mind doesn't understand abstract thoughts or terms—it needs visuals. It needs to recognize what is happening and so, on a video, for example, you would say you see yourself doing this, that, and the other, and it's all visual and clear. You can see the action happening, whatever that is. And I would say choose three video events, not just one, because three visuals will be very important for you and your subconscious mind to recognize that these events have already taken place.

Now, for example, you can't say, "I feel joyful." The video will not capture that. Seeing you joyful would perhaps mean seeing you smiling ear to ear, laughing, jumping up and down, punching the air, and hugging somebody tight.

b. Auditory

How will your subconscious mind know that you've achieved your goal? How would you know? What will you hear?

The subconscious mind will want to hear what people are saying about you having achieved your goal. It wants to know who specifically you are hearing say, "Congratulations!" and "Well done!"

The action has already happened. You have already achieved what you set out to do. Now, we know you haven't, but remember, your subconscious mind doesn't know the difference between reality and fantasy. You're building the foundation and the rail tracks to your dream and the subconscious mind will find it, and it will take you there, but you must help it believe that you have already arrived.

Equally important is, what will you be saying to yourself now that you've achieved your dream? What is your inner dialogue? "Oh! My God, I've done it!" "I can't believe it!" or "Yes, it's done!" Whatever it is you say to yourself, you must hear it said, because it is received by the subconscious in a different way, and it reinforces the message it receives from the visual and the kinesthetic.

c. Kinesthetic

How will your subconscious mind know that you've achieved your goal? How would you know? What will you feel?

How do you really feel now that your dream has come true? What does it make you feel? This is important. And then you need to drill down on this feeling. This joy—or whatever feeling you have, having achieved this dream—have you felt it before? And if you have felt it before, how did it feel? Where did you feel it in your body? If that feeling has a color, what is it? If it has a shape, what is it? What about texture? When you touch it with your hands, how does it feel?

Now, these are details that are important and specific, because your subconscious mind will find ways to achieve your goal before it's achieved it. It's very much like the quantum world. You're creating something that's not there yet and you bring it into creation. The subconscious mind is like a tape player: unless you change the tape, it will not change. Now, make certain that you sear what you've seen, heard, and felt into your subconscious mind by repeating it until it materializes.

★   ★   ★

6

REBEL PURPOSE

"The unexamined life is not worth living."

—Socrates (470–399 BC)
Greek Philosopher

An unexamined life is not worth living. What did Socrates mean? I suspect that, like me, you have spent years doing what was expected of you. Yet when confronted by a serious illness or our mortality, we start to question everything. After my encounter with death back in January 2007, I started examining my life and it's been a continuous journey for me since then. For many, when faced with retirement, which is a crisis, they ponder on this question: what is my purpose now? What is it I want to be doing before I move on from this world? What is it that I haven't yet done?

This is, if you like, life giving you a heads-up, a wake-up call to start living your dream now, before it's too late. It's your last chance, so don't waste this opportunity. It changes the way you look at this stage of life. Instead of tiptoeing to a quiet death, you should be going out with a bang. Because what else is life for?

Life Lessons

Dr. Elisabeth Kübler-Ross, a Swiss-American psychologist, spent decades interviewing hundreds of people on their deathbeds. She wrote several books including *Life Lessons* and *On Death and Dying* and, in a nutshell, what she discovered was that a significant percentage of people who were dying had not accomplished their dreams, and they were angry and resentful at not having done so.

Like most people, they'd been following what other people had told them to do, whether it was parents, spouses, partners, or siblings. They never did what they wanted to do. They always put other people first, thinking that what they were doing was a virtuous act. Now this is a shame because it's almost as if they had wasted their lives. Each of us is given an opportunity to do something in this life, and we stop ourselves because we put others first. When we put our lover, our family, or whatever it is that stops us pursuing what we should be doing, we betray ourselves.

Doing other people's bidding all the time is not love—neither on your part nor on those who love you. The Christian saying, "Love your neighbor as yourself," is much misunderstood. This saying has two parts. The first part is "Love your neighbor." The second part is "as yourself," which assumes you love yourself. Those who put others first, with no thought for themselves, are in fact negating this saying. They are in fact behaving as though the saying was "Love your neighbor, instead of yourself." To highlight this misunderstanding, I reverse the saying and put this question to you: If you don't love yourself, how can you love your neighbor? It's impossible, isn't it?

We are all meant to excel at what we do, and it's written in our very DNA, writes Richard Bolles, author of the perennial bestseller, *What Color Is Your Parachute?* "Your purpose is written in your DNA. It's written in the way you live, the way you talk, whatever you do, it's there for you to see it. You just need to open your eyes and wake up."

Dr. Kübler-Ross had a devil of a time trying to get doctors to understand what she was doing, and they resented her for talking to the dying. What she discovered from the dying is that they knew they were dying, even though the doctors and the nurses wouldn't talk about it. In fact, the dying knew from the reactions of the doctors and nurses that they were dying, because of the way the medics started to slowly switch off from them. Most of the dying finally accept their situation and let go, but some who die, don't. Now that you're facing retirement or if you're already in retirement and want to un-retire, you need to give thought to this question: what is your purpose? What is it that you must do, and have not yet done? What do you really, really want to do, before you die?

You need to spend time on this because you're worth it. You need to spend time with yourself to discover what it is that you're meant to do with the rest of your life.

In search of meaning

Our search for meaning is not a luxury, or something wonderful to do, but a necessity. It is as essential to our mind as food and water are to our bodies. One man who understood this at a fundamental level was Viktor Frankl, a neurologist, psychiatrist, and author. He was an Austrian Jew who lost his wife, his family, his children, and his friends at Auschwitz in the 1940s. His manuscript was also taken away from him, and he almost lost his life too. He was an individual with a deep sense of purpose. Even in the most dire circumstances of his life, he made it his purpose to help his fellow men. In his book, *Man's Search for Meaning*, he talks about his life, his family, his experiences, and his purpose. After the end of World War II, he crafted a study called Logotherapy—all related to this concept of purpose and meaning in life, without which he believed we humans perish.

Frankl suggests that we ask ourselves three simple questions:

1. What is it that you give of yourself in life, in terms of the service you provide?

2. What do you take from life, in terms of experiences?

3. When life throws you into unpleasant circumstances, what is the stand you take, and do you stand up for what is right?

That stand that you take, in whatever situation, is your choice. Why? Because we each pick our battles. After all, we can't fight every battle. Yet, the battle that you choose to fight, the stand you choose to take, is crucially important, because that's where you find the meaning of your life.

Purpose and meaning of life are not the same thing. The meaning of life focuses on the significance of life, and it's a psychological concept. Purpose, on the other hand, has a spiritual aspect, and is more like a journey or a course of action. When you are passionate about something, you feel an emotional connection to it, and it drives you to find your true calling.

Worthy Purpose and Self-Understanding

So how do we discover our worthy purpose and how do we get self-understanding?

Paul Wong, a Chinese Canadian psychologist, came up with four elements that constitute purpose and meaning in life.

The first element you need is a worthy purpose. Not just any purpose, but a worthy purpose on two levels. It must be worthy from deep within you, in the sense that it has emotional value to you. It must also be worthy from without (from the outside), meaning something ambitious. You need to stretch yourself to reach it. A worthy purpose serves a double purpose, and that's what makes it sustainable.

In my case, I had to think very deeply about what my purpose was. Initially, my purpose was to help people develop their mindsets, and I didn't have a target market. I was offering my services to all—male and female, all ages, all socio-economic levels—which meant I was serving no one in particular. I clearly couldn't serve everyone, so I had to go back to the drawing board and find out who I wanted to serve above all. Now believe me, baby boomers were my last choice. I instinctively avoided them because to be very honest and upfront, they are so reluctant to change and they are not the easiest of tribes. They don't like change. They like to stay where they are. They like the "good old days." I am as sentimental as the next person, but I don't like the "good old days." I think it is a figment of our imagination. We're very selective about our memories. When we refer to the "good old days," what does it say about us? Does it not imply that our best days were in the past? And if that's the case, are we not confessing that our present and our future are bleak?

So, why is it that I ultimately chose the retiring baby boomer market? Well, first, because I'm one of the tribe. Baby boomers are my tribe. I understand them, I know where they came from, and I can help them because I've been on this journey myself. So, my purpose now is to help retiring baby boomers "un-retire" and create a new life for themselves, because given that we may have another 20 or 30 years of life, that's a hell of a long time to drift aimlessly.

The second element is understanding who you are. Most of us don't understand who we are. We wake up in the morning, we brush our teeth, have our coffee, our breakfast, and we go to work. We do our work, our errands, we come back home and ultimately, we go to sleep and our day is over. The next day is the same thing all over again. We don't stop to think, what am I doing? Who am I?

What's more, we're not who we think we are. We have many masks. We've created many masks from our childhood. When we were young, we couldn't lie well, and so our lies would be exposed. As we got older, we became better at lying, and we developed a second skin, a new identity. Who you really are isn't the mask you present to different people: to your family, your siblings, your friends, or your professional network. Who you really are is the vulnerable self within you, the person that you prefer not to expose to anybody out there, for fear of what they might say. So, it's getting to know who you really are—the person behind the mask.

The Greek word for mask is "persona." We wear different personas throughout our lives. In retirement, we have the opportunity to take off our masks, and to be who we truly are. It's a difficult thing to do. It's a frightening thing to do, but we must do it, because if we don't do it now, when will we start living our true lives? Do we want to be taking off our masks on our deathbed?

Are you ready to understand who you really are? Are you ready to take off your mask now, to become the real you, the vulnerable you, and to start to feel again? Are you brave enough to do that? I know you are, because if I can do it, you can do it. Believe me, I used to be fearful. Not anymore. So, I know you can do it because I did.

The third element is that you alone are responsible. This is hugely important. For a long time, I was doing what I was supposed to be doing. I had deluded myself into believing that I was doing what I wanted to do, but that wasn't the case. The reality was that I'd been programmed, and I was comfortable under that security blanket, so why would I want to change? To discover ourselves, we need to take off our masks. We need to take off our armor. And when we take off our armor, we become vulnerable, which allows us to be open and engage with other people at a genuine level.

If we take off our masks, will we not be hurt again? Of course we will, but it doesn't matter anymore because the hurt is short-lived, while the joy lasts so much longer, and we are worth every bit of that experience. So, recognize that you, and you alone, are responsible. Now you must bear in mind that nobody is going to decide for you to change your life. You're in charge, you're the pilot, you're the captain of your ship. You alone must make that decision. Nobody else is going to make that decision for you. Your spouse won't make it, your parents aren't going to make it, your children aren't going to make it. You must take that responsibility, and it is a responsibility, but it's fine. You can do it. Take the responsibility of changing your life to follow your dream. You only get one shot at this—possibly your last shot, so don't wait for permission, because it won't come. The persons who could have given you permission are probably long gone.

In case you're like I was, I'm going to give you permission, because I was given permission. Yes, it's bizarre that some of us baby boomers need permission. We need permission not because we're stupid; we need permission because that's how we've been programmed and (unknowingly) we're unaware that we've been programmed to seek permission. While we know in our conscious mind that it's a silly idea, our subconscious mind is waiting for permission. It's a self-sabotaging program. That may be one of the programs you need to get rid of, so don't judge yourself. You have been given permission, so proceed, without delay.

The fourth element is that if you have a worthy purpose, an understanding of who you are, and you take responsibility for your decisions, you will enjoy a deep sense of significance and satisfaction.

Ikigai: Life Purpose

The Japanese word "*ikigai*" is often translated as "the purpose of life." *Ikigai* can encompass your life purpose, but the word is usually used to indicate things that make one's life worth living. On a deeper level, *ikigai* refers to the emotional circumstances under which individuals feel that their lives are valuable as they move forward towards their goals. Finding *ikigai* is the process of cultivating your inner potential as you actively pursue what you enjoy doing in service of your family, tribe, and community, through your roles in life.

The Westernized version of *ikigai* is based on the idea that there are four components one needs to complete to achieve *ikigai*.

The four components are represented by the four questions:

- Are you doing an activity that you love?
- Are you good at what you do?
- Does the world need what you offer?
- Can you get paid for doing it?

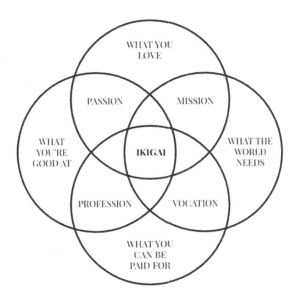

The misconception that's perpetuated is that you can only achieve *ikigai* and true joy by meeting all four conditions, so if you're doing what you love to do, but you are not generating any money, then you have not achieved *ikigai*. This is patently false.

The four questions in the framework are not questions that the Japanese ask themselves when they are contemplating their *ikigai*. If a native Japanese were to be shown this Venn diagram, they would not recognize it as *ikigai*.

The credit for the creation of the Venn diagram of "Purpose" goes to Spanish author and psychological astrologer, Andrés Zuzunaga, who featured it in Borja Vilaseca's book *Qué Harías Si No Tuvieras Miedo (What Would You Do If You Weren't Afraid?)* published in 2012. Eventually, it was translated into English and was used by life coaches as a simplistic overview to find purpose in your career.

For some people this works perfectly well, as it did for me, but you just have to remember this is not the authentic Japanese *ikigai*. To best understand how the Japanese define *ikigai*, we refer to Japanese neuroscientist Ken Mogi, author of *The Little Book of Ikigai* and *Awakening Your Ikigai*. The supportive framework that Mogi proposes in his books are the "Five Pillars" that he believes allow *ikigai* to flourish, and they are:

1. Starting small
2. Releasing yourself
3. Harmony and sustainability
4. The joy of little things
5. Being in the here and now

Clearly, in my view, the Western transplanted approach to *ikigai* will work well enough for many retired and retiring baby boomers, but I think that they could gain so much more by the application of the Japanese *ikigai*, which offers us a deeper understanding of finding our purpose in starting small, finding joy in the small things, and above all, living in the present moment.

Have you examined your life? Are you living a worthwhile life? When you discover your life purpose, your investment in this book will have paid off, not a hundred fold, but perhaps as much as a hundred thousand fold.

★   ★   ★

DISCOVER

ASSIMILATE

REWIRE

EXPAND

7

THE GRATITUDE REBEL

"Thankfulness is the pathway into Thinking."

—Martin Heidegger (1889–1976)
German philosopher

What does "gratitude" have to do with mindset?

The answer is everything. If you're not grateful for what you already have, it doesn't matter how much work you do, how much money you make, or how important you become, because you'll never be happy. If you're not happy and thankful inside, what's the point? We're not animals; we're thinking human beings. Therefore, if you're grateful for what you have, it also opens the possibility for new things to come into your life.

Being thankful is an integral part of thinking. Gratitude is not what you might think or might have heard. It is not to be confused with the meaning of gratitude, which you may have been taught in your early years by your parents or teachers. That is more about social skills. Nor is it what many people today think of as a "woo-hoo" thing—a wonderful state of mind, but in practice, it's not going to add to your income (which is untrue). Gratitude is pivotal to a change of mindset. In fact, gratitude is linked to our thinking and if we're not grateful, we're not thinking.

Let's take a step back into antiquity. Cicero, the Roman states-man, lawyer, and writer, was an amazing and articulate individual who spoke up for democracy and the rule of law. He stood up to Julius Caesar and all forms of tyranny. US President John Adams, a signer of the US Constitution, credits Cicero's writings for having a profound influence on the drafting of the US Consti-tution. Cicero had this to say about gratitude: "Gratitude is not only the greatest of virtues, but the parent of all the others."

Now why would Cicero say that?

Cicero was a man of the world, so why would he rate grati-tude so highly? Wouldn't gratitude be seen as a weakness in the cruel world of Rome? I think it's because Cicero must have understood that gratitude and thinking were interlinked. In my view, cultivating an attitude of gratitude elevates us, gives us altitude, and elevates our consciousness.

How did I reach this conclusion?

The power of a word and thought

In his research on the word "gratitude," German philosopher Martin Heidegger dug deep to understand the essence of the words "gratitude" and "thankfulness." He discovered a surprising fact about a specific proto-German word, *thanken*, and the old English word *thanc*, meaning "a grateful thought." His research revealed that linguistically, the root of the words "thinking" and "thanking" are derived from the same word, *thanken* or *thanc*.

Heidegger expands:

"The *thanc* means man's inmost mind, the heart, the heart's core, that inmost essence of man which reaches outward most fully and to the outermost limits, and so decisively that, rightly considered, the idea of an inner and outer world does not arise … in giving thanks, the heart in thought recalls where it remains gathered and concentrated, because that is where it belongs."

He surmised that in the Middle Ages, when life was precarious and nothing could be taken for granted, people were inclined to pray and be thankful for their daily crust of bread. In his view, thinking and thanking must have co-existed as a pair. Heidegger's interpretation was that *"thankfulness is the pathway into thinking,"* and the reason for this is that if you're not thankful, you're not thinking properly.

Just because your mind is processing all sorts of things, it doesn't mean you're thinking. Nobel Prize-winning Danish physicist Niels Bohr captured the essence of this when he famously quipped: "No, no, no, you're not thinking; you're just being logical." It's having a sense of gratitude that makes you think correctly. So, for example, if you're thankful about what you already have, it puts you in the right state of mind. If you're grateful for your family, for your spouse, for your children, for the roof over your head, for the water you drink, for your life, your purpose, everything you have—if you're grateful for all of that, it means you're thinking correctly. You're not a slave to your whims, so you're not going to do anything stupid because you're thinking correctly.

Imagine how nice it is to work with somebody who's grateful to work with you, as opposed to somebody who's ungrateful. Imagine how many new possibilities open for you at work if you're grateful. People don't generally like ungrateful people. We're not attracted to ungrateful people. So, cultivating an attitude of gratitude gives us altitude. It raises our consciousness. The attitude of gratitude opens opportunities for us.

Now you hear a lot of people talking about manifestation. Well, manifesting is not a new thing. Manifesting goes back at least 2000 years. Jesus talked about it. In Mark 11:24, Jesus declares, "Therefore I tell you, whatever you ask for in prayer, believe that you have received it, and it will be yours." That's what faith is about. You believe you have already received it and you're thankful for it. So, you're in that grateful mindset, you're in that quantum field. You're already in possession of that thing because you are grateful for it.

When our minds are constantly looking at our past memories, our "good old days," we are stuck and we cannot move forward. The only way forward is to create a future memory of what we desire (our purpose), which we then manifest in the present. So, when we manifest what we desire, and we're grateful for it, and we believe that we've already received it, it puts us into that quantum field of having received it. This is science, not magic, or just wishful thinking.

One final point on this is that when we align our "thinking" and "thanking," we create a magnetic alignment. If we're not thankful, our mind is all over the place. It is not aligned and not focused. When our "thinking" and "thanking" are aligned, we automatically attract what we desire.

Religions and Cultures agree on one thing

Most religions disagree on most things. There are very few things that religions do agree on, and one of them is gratitude. All religions teach an aspect of gratitude, and it is contained not just in the religion itself, but in the culture of the people who abide within that religion.

Let's take Hinduism as an example. Hinduism teaches to *"give without expectation,"* and the reason you should give without expectation is not for the benefit of the other person, but for your own benefit (the benefit of the giver). If you have an expectation attached to the giving and you don't receive back, you're going to be frustrated and miserable. What was the point of giving in the first place?

For Buddhists, gratitude is an attitude of mind that must be cultivated because it softens a hardened heart. It allows for forgiveness and allows clarity of mind for spiritual growth. For Buddhists, gratitude is also the antidote to greed, lust, and all the other vices. Lastly, for Buddhists, when they give donations to their monastic communities, it is a form of gratitude for the services that the monks provide to them.

In Judaism, gratitude plays a huge role. For example, when we look at the book of Psalms, there are numerous psalms full of thanksgiving for the things that God has given his people. With the Jews, in fact, the very name Judah, from which the word "Jew" is derived, means thanksgiving. When the mother of Judah gave birth, she gave him the name Judah as a way of thanking God for giving her a son. And for the Jews, gratitude has a special place because they have many festivals celebrating it, Passover being one of them. The Passover meal is a meal of thanksgiving for saving them from slavery in Egypt. And lastly, and most interestingly, gratitude isn't something that's temporal for the Jews: it has no expiry date.

Gratitude has no expiry date. Why? Because if it's linked to thinking, how could it expire? If you're not always grateful, you're not always thinking. Gratitude has no expiry date for that very reason, if nothing else.

For Christians, the Eucharist is considered a sacrament and is essential in their worship. And the word Eucharist itself is derived from the Greek word *eucharistia*, meaning thanksgiving, so as you can see, thanksgiving is not only an essential practice, but is also considered a virtue. It's a virtue that is to be applied not only in thought and spirit, but also in action.

The apostle Paul writes that we should be thankful even for "our sufferings because we know that suffering produces perseverance; perseverance, character; and character, hope. And hope does not put us to shame, because God's love has been poured out into our hearts through the Holy Spirit, who has been given to us" (Romans 5:3–5).

In other words, we should be grateful for the crises in our lives, because they open opportunities for us that would not otherwise have been available.

Lastly, in Islam, they have a practice called *Shukr*—meaning thanksgiving. No prayer is complete without the *Shukr*. *Shukr* appears in the Quran many times. Another aspect in Islam where

they consider thanksgiving essential is during the feast of Rama-
dan where they go fasting for a whole month. An interesting
point to note is that the Muslim expression *Alhamdulillah* means
praise and thanks be to God, and Muslims use it constantly in
their conversations.

The Science of Gratitude

Dr. Robert Emmons, Professor of Psychology at the University of California at Davis, has studied and researched gratitude
extensively, and he's affectionately known as the "Gratitude Professor." He has written numerous books, including *The Little
Book of Gratitude, The Psychology of Gratitude, Thanks, Words of
Gratitude,* and *Gratitude Works.* Dr. Emmons proposes four reasons why gratitude is scientifically good for us.

The first is that gratitude magnifies everything that we have.
For example, if we have a spouse, a partner, a child, a home, or
a car, and we're grateful for them, then we're deriving pleasure
because we're enjoying what we already have. When we're not
grateful for what we have, then there's no joy in it because our
focus is elsewhere. We're thinking about getting something else,
then another thing, and then another. We need to be constantly
doing to get some happiness out of the searching and the pur-
chase of something new. The quest is never-ending because the
void inside us is impossible to satisfy. Conversely, if we value what
we buy, and we're grateful for it, it magnifies what we bought,
and we don't feel the need to constantly go out and buy stuff.

The second thing is that gratitude blocks toxic emotions like
pride, gluttony, greed, anger, envy, lust, and despair. If we don't
believe it, all we need to do is try to be grateful about something
and then try to have a toxic emotion. It's impossible to have both
because they are like oil and water. They don't mix, so being

grateful blocks all these toxic emotions which are not good for us. Remember, every time we have a toxic thought, it releases toxic chemicals into our bodies. Remember the firing and wiring of our neurons? So, it's not about doing anybody else a favor, it's about doing ourselves a favor. Avoid toxic emotions by using its antidote: gratitude.

The third point is that gratitude helps us deal with stress because it blocks it. When we're grateful, we're unlikely to be stressed. For example, you're driving your car and another car cuts you off unexpectedly from a side road. Your immediate reaction is to get furious. You go into a rage. Now these thoughts start to release toxic messages to your body. You're feeding your anger, but you're addicted to this feeling, so you're also enjoying this drama. Now imagine the next time somebody cuts you off on the road. You're aware of your automatic reactions, but this time you've created and prepared a new response. Your new thought in response to this event is that the person in that car is desperate for whatever reason, perhaps to get to the hospital because his child has been involved in an accident. This new story you tell yourself will change your mindset. You let the man go in peace. You are grateful for your lot in life. Do this a few times and the anger will disappear. Gratitude also makes you more stress resilient when you are unwell and helps you recuperate much faster.

The fourth point is that gratitude strengthens social ties and self-worth. When we're grateful, people appreciate us. People love to be thanked for what they do, and if we pick up on that, we've won them over. When people start appreciating us, that increases our self-worth in our own eyes. So, being grateful works like the magic of compound interest; the benefits grow in size and in speed.

Gratitude should be understood not only in terms of science but also in terms of spirituality. It's linked to our thinking, and it improves our lives immeasurably. So why wouldn't we want to be grateful if it's going to enhance and expand our lives? Gratitude opens up a quantum field of opportunities that would not have been there for us, that we could not have seen or been aware of.

We all need to cultivate gratitude. It will not just happen on its own. We need to cultivate it daily with the people that we love and the people we work with. So, let's use gratitude to elevate our consciousness, and it'll improve our lives immeasurably.

Once you make this transformation, your retired friends may not be pleased about this new change in you. You will be a threat to their old way of life, which of course you are. In fact, they will do everything to pull you back into their group thinking. You have to be very careful about this. Do not react. Understand their situation and approach it differently. What you need to do is be strong enough to pull away from them at first. Eventually, you may bring some of them to your camp because you're the one who's right and you know that. So don't fall back into your old ways and play it safe. You need to be a leader. You need to be a rebel. That is how you will help your family and friends.

Have faith. Whatever you ask in prayer, believe that you have already received it, and it will be yours.

★   ★   ★

8

REBEL WITH A CAUSE

"Rebels are people who break rules that should be broken. They break rules that hold them and others back, and their way of rule breaking is constructive rather than destructive."

—Dr. Francesca Gino
Harvard Business School professor and
author of *Rebel Talent*

So how do you become a "rebel with a cause"?
We become a "rebel with a cause" when we:

1. Break retirement rules that should be broken.

2. Break the power of fear and grow the power of love.

3. Break free of the old mindset and understand the difference between knowing and doing.

1. Break Retirement Rules That Should Be Broken

We need to break retirement rules and create a positive change in our lives. Firstly, I would break the retirement age of 65. Why not retire at the age of 90?

Originally, when the retirement age of 65 was initiated by German Chancellor Bismarck in the 1870s, life expectancy was 58 at that time. So, by extending the retirement age a full seven years, a clear buffer was created to allow those who survived to age 65 and beyond to have the financial security available to them. In 2020, life expectancy for men and women in the UK and in the US is 83 years of age. If we use the Bismarck model, we should add seven years to the age of 83, which would give us a new retirement age of 90. In reality, 90 should be the new retirement age, given that we now have a good 25 years (90 less 65) of life left to live. This is a politically explosive subject, and that is why no politician or political party will touch it, and it's also why financial services firms are unable to offer non-financial solutions because they are constricted by regulatory authorities.

Take a minute and consider this scenario. If you did retire at 65, how would you fund the next 25 years and more? Where would your money come from? Whatever savings you have most likely won't take you to the age of ninety, so you are likely to outlive your savings. In fact, the worst case scenario is that when you reach your 80s, your assets will have depleted considerably or totally, just when you need money the most, because of medical and nursing bills. Also, because in your 80s, you would, in all probability, have been retired for some time, you would not be fit to return to work of any kind. What will you do then? I hope that I have managed to persuade you that the whole concept of retirement at 65 is irrational and impractical, and yet millions upon millions of people still look at 65 as their retirement age. My message to those thinking of retiring before the age of 90 is the same warning that Dante, the author of *The Divine Comedy*, wrote at the entrance of hell: "Abandon all hope, ye who enter here."

We, as rebels, know better. We know we can't retire. We don't dwell on it. We don't dream about it. We don't feel that we're missing out on it. We are far from it. We need to create a new dynamic, a new purpose in our lives. We need to harness that purpose with passion and that will keep us healthy, because we'll be engaged socially and on a personal level.

In the previous chapters, we've learned how to change our mindsets. We know how our mind works (particularly our subconscious mind) and now we've tried to change it, but we need to recognize that it's not going to happen quickly. We need to recognize that we need to repeat and then take action. Without action, nothing will take place.

Why repeat? Because our subconscious mind seeks confirmation through repetition. The more we repeat, the more solid our new plan becomes, and the less likely we are to drop back to our previous thinking. Like a spider throws a filament out repeatedly until it's strong, think of your dream and turn it into a vision. Then bring it into reality by fortifying it with your emotions.

You know what to do. You need to apply it so that you can make it concrete for your subconscious mind. You've also learnt about the power of your intellectual faculties, using your imagination. Don't underestimate the power of your imagination. No, it's not fantasy. Look around you. Everything you see that is not a living organism was created and made by human imagination. Your desk, your chair, your bed, your pen and paper, your smartphone, your laptop, your watch, your books, your home, your office, and so on. These are not fantasies. Imagination is imagination, and the reason you're receiving those visions is because it's there for you to use it, so don't knock it and don't put yourself down. Release the need for approval from your family and friends, whose company you've probably outgrown. You cannot and must not wait for approval from your family and friends. Do you want to wait until you're on your deathbed before you realize you have a dream to fulfill?

Use that imagination, harness it, and write it down.

Writing has magic. When you write something down, you're creating it. In fact, it's already semi-created because whilst it's in your imagination, it's still an idea and yet it can vanish, and might not come back. The minute you write it down, you make it real.

Think of architects—they have an image of what a building's going to look like. They put it down on paper, by drawing a blueprint, and then they build it. By downloading the image from their minds onto a blueprint, they have breathed life into a two-dimensional idea; they have made it real. And that's what writing does for you. You need to physically write it out. Also ensure that you use all your senses because the subconscious mind will start activating when you bring your sensory feelings into your writing.

Finally, gratitude. Gratitude is what opens this new quantum field for you that you didn't know existed. It reminds me of the story of Alexander Luria, the young Soviet Russian neuropsychologist who went out to Uzbekistan in the 1930s to test out what the Uzbek peasants understood about abstract concepts such as circles, squares, and triangles. The peasants couldn't understand the concept of circles, squares, and triangles. They only saw what they thought was real to them: a circle was the sun or the moon; a square was a house or a barn; a triangle was a mountain. The idea of abstract concepts was beyond their understanding; it was alien to their culture. Similarly, people today don't understand the concept of quantum fields or quantum physics. It's an alien concept until we raise our consciousness to understand what it is and how it works, and then we can appreciate that our previous thinking was not as real as we thought.

So, use gratitude to elevate your consciousness. It will work magic. Dovetail it with your thinking, and it'll deliver the results you seek.

2. Break the Power of Fear and Grow the Power of Love

The second rule that needs to be broken is the power of fear. The way to become a rebel with a cause is to use the power of love. You may recall from earlier chapters that I touched on the work of Dr. Elisabeth Kubler-Ross, the author of *On Death and Dying* and *Life Lessons*. One of the things she discovered was that there are only two basic human emotions: fear and love. For most of us here on this planet, fear plays a huge role. We're fearful of this and fearful of that. People are either going to kill us, steal from us, or harm us. We're constantly under the oppression of fear, which allows no room for love. Why? Because fear and love are like oil and water: they don't mix.

We're either living in the field of fear or in the field of love. Love causes us huge amounts of anxiety, because we would naturally choose love, but we're afraid of the consequences, and the pain of loss. We live our lives mostly in a state of fear because we're fearful to live in joy and love, scared that if/when we lose them, we'll experience the pain of loss. So, we spend year after year existing in fear instead of living a life of love. Imagine if we lived in a state of joy year after year, and occasionally experienced fear. Isn't that preferable? Isn't that a more intelligent choice?

Now, as we hit the magical age of 60 or 65, we enter our third age. We've spent most of our lives in fear, chasing the buck, and now we have an opportunity to live our lives the way we would like to live. That's when we need to reject fear and focus on love, because with love, everything starts to open for us. Yes, we become more vulnerable, but equally more powerful, and we can live the lives we were meant to lead.

Are you not tired of being afraid?

At our stage in life, what do you have to lose?

Do you want to have a joyful life?

You wouldn't be reading this book if you didn't have a rebel bone in you. So, you don't need to be afraid. You don't want to die with your dream still inside you. Use the power of love to nourish your dream. The whole purpose of your life was to implement your dream. Use your dream or lose it.

3. Break Free of the Old Mindset

The third rule that needs to be broken is the old mindset. To become a rebel with a cause is to understand the difference between knowing and doing.

"Knowing" is the arena of the conscious mind. "Doing" is the arena of the subconscious. "Knowing" has the facility to slide off our mind, like Teflon, whereas "Doing" has the facility to stick hard in our mind, like Velcro.

The challenge is that despite knowing what to do, we don't do it. Despite knowing who we really are, we allow some stranger to knock us off course. Despite all the wisdom, knowledge, and information, we still don't apply it. Knowledge is not king; applied knowledge is king. It is converting knowledge into action. We know so much that is true, but because this knowledge touches our conscious mind, it slides off our mind, much like Teflon. Until we "experience" that which is true, we will not understand it. Why? Because through the process of experiencing it, this knowledge touches our subconscious mind, our emotional mind, and this knowledge sticks hard to us, much like Velcro.

Just think of the last non-fiction book you read. You pick up a few ideas from that book and you try to retain it in your memory. You think you're going to retain it, but it vanishes. I read a lot of books and even though I can't retain a lot, I can still remember some salient nuggets, which I need to use in my work or teaching. If I don't write it down, it slides off like Teflon. Our mind processes information very fast and only keeps the things it needs to. If you want to remember a fact or a story, you need to attach an emotional molecule to it, or a feeling to it. Much of what we "know" just slides off our mind, whereas much of what we "do" repeatedly attaches itself to our subconscious.

Therefore, rebels know that they must work hard on repetition, persistence, and taking action. Because if you don't act, no result will ensue, and you'll have wasted your time. I repeat this, ad nauseam, because it's so important and I want you to succeed.

A perfect example is Lucy Kellaway, a former *Financial Times* journalist who became a teacher in her 50s. Although she went through some trials and tribulations, she never once wished to be back in her old familiar background. In an article in *The Guardian* newspaper on July 14, 2021, she wrote:

> "My generation was brought up to think that we would do one thing and when we had made enough money or got tired of it, we would stop working altogether. Some of my professional contemporaries have started building portfolio existences and do a bit of this and a bit of that, but the more obvious route—an entirely new career—is still a rarity. This is not because people don't want to start again, but because no one is showing them how."[2]

Well, here you are, and you've been shown the why and the how.

Your life script

You can create your own life script. In my program, Dare to Discover Your Purpose, I offer exercises in each of the eight modules that build on each other and ultimately you can collate all of them to create your own life script. I always suggest that you write your script in your own handwriting because

---

[2] The Guardian 14 July 2021 – Leaving burnout behind: the pain and pleasure of starting a new career in my 50s – https://amp-theguardian-com.cdn.ampproject.org/c/s/amp.theguardian.com/education/2021/jul/14/leaving-burnout-behind-the-pain-and-pleasure-of-starting-a-new-career-in-my-50s?fbclid=IwAR1o0xtasaiERxNCjrx egxM9Hxa_qeAd_9rLB_1LBsgA5eQItUKSW7R49AA

writing has magic imbued in it. The physical act of writing creates a neural connection with our minds, which typing cannot achieve. The act of writing creates something that wasn't there; it makes it come to life. So write out your script (and your script can be several pages or distilled down to one page).

Once you have done the first edit, leave it for a few days. Come back to it and take time out in a quiet place. Take deep breaths. Slow yourself down and go into a meditative state. Don't think. Focus on your breath, in and out. Now edit your script. Ensure that all verbs are in the present tense, not past and future tenses. Use the personal pronoun "I" and keep your sentences short. Use emotionally charged verbs and words so the subconscious mind can pick up on that feeling immediately.

Review your script, your blueprint, and ensure that each sentence is injected with love, and with the intention of love, and always in the present tense. Now that your future blueprint is mapped out, you must breathe life into it by aligning it with your feelings. Feelings are the secret sauce, which provides your blueprint with oxygen to breathe. So go over your script again, and harness your feelings to each sentence, wherever you can, with emotional verbs that resonate with you. Now your blueprint can take off like a rocket.

There are three ways that you can impress your blueprint onto your subconscious mind. You can use a voice recording of your script. This may take a few months, but it can be sooner. You can use hypnosis, which will be faster. Lastly, you can use the PSYCH-K® method which, in my view, is the fastest of all. Whichever way you choose, you must act. Without taking action, nothing will happen.

Voice recording

Once your script is ready, read it repeatedly to yourself, morning and evening, and you will feel your body absorbing your script by osmosis. You can also record it on voice memo or voice-loop apps, which is my preference. Record your script and play it to yourself first thing in the morning and last thing at night. At night before sleeping is an ideal time, when your conscious mind is slowing down, and your subconscious mind is awakening. Another ideal time is in the morning, just before your subconscious mind recedes, and before your conscious mind is fully awakened.

These are the perfect times to drop this information into your subconscious mind. And your subconscious mind will act. You don't have to think about the "how." The action your subconscious takes will be better and faster than what your conscious mind can ever devise.

Hypnosis

Hypnosis gets a bad rap, which it doesn't deserve. Some people have a distrust of hypnosis. That said, I believe that hypnosis is an excellent way to connect with the subconscious. I would recommend you go to a hypnotherapist you know. There are plenty of people out there who will be able to help put you in a state of mind where your subconscious can receive and absorb your script. Don't forget this is your script, your information, and your dream. You have nothing to fear; you can allow your subconscious mind to absorb it.

PSYCH-K®

In my view, PSYCH-K® is a proven and safe way to change subconscious beliefs that perpetuate old habits of thinking and behaving that you would like to change. Developed about 25 years ago in New Mexico by Dr. Rob Williams, PSYCH-K® became popular when cell biologist Dr. Bruce Lipton experienced a profound change in his life because of it, and he now works very closely with Dr. Rob Williams. PSYCH-K® is phenomenal in the way that it delivers results in very little time, but again, it requires action. If you don't act, it won't happen.

Most of us are either left-brained or right-brained, and very few of us are whole-brained. So, for most of us, it's almost like living life with one hand behind our backs. What Psych-K® offers is to integrate the left and right hemispheres of our brain through physical muscle testing and non-physical muscle testing.

You can find a PSYCH-K® facilitator anywhere near you by going to https://psych-k.com/about/ and either look for the nearest facilitator to you or one that appeals to you. You don't need to see them physically, as most work online.

In the autumn of our lives, just as in nature, our true colors emerge. So let's embrace our new life, our new purpose, passion, and potential, and become Rebels with a Cause.

★   ★   ★

CONCLUSION

While life and nature are all about constant change, human nature resists it as an automatic reflex. Change terrifies most people. Very few people like change, and even those who do are generally happy for others to change, but resent having to change or transform themselves.

Imagine how the industrial revolution of the 19th century ushered in a period of social, economic, and political changes that transformed individuals, families, societies, countries, and the world at large. Now imagine specifically how mechanization in the 1780s, electrification in the 1870s, automation in the 1970s, globalization in the 1980s, and digitalization today have changed our lives so irreversibly. We may wish to go back to the imagined idyllic world of yesterday, but that is gone forever. We can only live in the present and push forward. Let's make our lives worthwhile—not just for ourselves, but for those we love.

In December 1862, during the Civil War, with his Emancipation Proclamation due to take effect in a few weeks, President Abraham Lincoln was struggling to maintain some sense of national meaning. What he wrote in his message to Congress gives us lessons on how we should handle our current crisis:

"The dogmas of the quiet past are inadequate to the stormy present. The occasion is piled high with difficulty, and we must rise with the occasion. As our case is new, so we must think anew, and act anew."

These words resonate with us today, as we emerge from a global pandemic, to face a world that is changing right in front of us. The dogmas of the quiet, pre-Covid world are inadequate for the stormy present, which is piled high with difficulties, and so we too must rise with the occasion. As our circumstances are different, we must think and act differently.

When you reflect on your journey through this book, you can see retirement with a different perspective. Retirement is certainly a crisis, a turning point. In a sense, it is life knocking on your door alerting you to wake up to the fact that this is your last chance to implement your dream before the lights go out.

I started on my life transformative journey in January 2007, when I was diagnosed with a bone tumor and given six months to live. Then, three weeks later, my death sentence was commuted to six months rest and recuperation after surgery. From that point onwards, I have been living on bonus time. It was only 10 years later, in August 2017, after attending a week-long event with Bob Proctor and Sandy Gallagher in Toronto that my life took a different turn. Why? Because I learned about mindset change, I found my tribe of forward-looking people, and I took action to change my life. It was slow to start, and it was hard, because I was going outside my comfort zone and I struggled with my old paradigms that were difficult to shift, but it was the right thing to do. I have no regrets.

Changing my mindset changed my life. As the late spiritual author Dr. Wayne Dyer used to say:

"If you change the way you look at things, the things
you look at change."

My perspective changed. I loved learning about our mind
and how powerful it is. I could not read enough books on it. I
devoured books from the ancient Romans like Cicero, Seneca,
and Marcus Aurelius; from the Eastern mystics like Rumi, Lao
Tzu, and Confucius; from the early self-help gurus, like James
Allen, Thomas Troward, Neville Goddard, Napoleon Hill, Norman Vincent Peale, and Dale Carnegie; from more recent self-
help gurus like Tony Robbins, Stephen Covey, Dr. Wayne Dyer,
and Eckhart Tolle; from scientists like Dr. Bruce Lipton, Dr. Joe
Dispenza, and Dr. Maxwell Maltz; from psychologists like Dr.
Elisabeth Kubler-Ross, Prof. Robert Emmons, and Dr. Carol
S. Dweck; and so many more. The more I learned, the more I
wanted to help people migrate from the old mindset to the new
mindset, from the old world to the new world. My purpose was
beginning to take shape.

I started my new venture in 2017, at the age of 62, and I
slowly sold out and exited from my other business ventures so
I could focus on this project. At first, I started helping anyone
and everyone. I soon realized that I needed to focus on a select
type of client, what marketers call my "avatar." Eventually, I
realized that the very people I needed to attract were people like
me, people my age, people who were part of the baby boomer
generation (those born between 1946 and 1964). As I was born
in 1955, I was right in the middle, a perfect position.

In mid-2018, I changed the direction of my new business,
with a view to serving my tribe of boomers. I created a new
eight-week program called "Dare to Discover Your Purpose." In
March 2019, after nine months of incubation, I released it, just

before the Covid-19 pandemic shut down the world. For the past two years, I have been engaged in writing blogs, creating podcasts, and creating videos, which I shared on social media. Now, with this book, I see myself as an "authority" on this new subject matter for people in their 60s who want to carve out a new chapter in their lives. For me, this is not the end of my journey; it is the end of the beginning of my journey. I trust the process and although I do not know where this journey will take me, I revel in the wonderful mystery that will unravel before me.

The fact that you have read to this point in my book is a testament that you have not wasted this crisis. You have grabbed the opportunity with both hands, and you are now starting on your new journey, discovering an activity that makes your heart sing, that makes you socially engaged, and above all, that gives you a sense of purpose in life. It's been my honor and my privilege to have been your mentor for this first part of your new journey, and for which I am immensely grateful. Now, as you embark on your journey, remember that the journey will take you, so go with the flow, and enjoy each day as though it is your last.

★　　★　　★

ACKNOWLEDGMENTS

My first debt of gratitude goes to Bob Proctor and Sandy Gallagher of Proctor Gallagher Institute for becoming my teachers when I (the student) was ready and for inspiring me to become a mindset mentor.

I'm grateful to Eleanor Tucker for the assistance she gave me in crafting and editing my 8-module program over a nine-month period in 2020 and 2021, and for completing it just before we went into lockdown in the UK.

I thank Emma Bond Forrester for her spark of genius in coming up with the name and acronym DARE for my process.

I thank Rhiane Kirkby for her first critical edit to this book, and Jayne Cherrington Cook for all the beautiful photos and quotes she has generated on my social media.

My special thanks go to Dan Twine for his high quality of work in shooting and editing my 8-module online course over a two-week period in March 2020, and for the excellent set of photographs that can now be seen on my website and book.

Enormous thanks to Janak and Urvi Mehta of Clients Online in Scottsdale, Arizona, for running my advertising campaigns across the UK, US, Canada, Australia, and New Zealand.

I am grateful to Nathan Householder of InfusionSoft Keap, who helps me manage my database, which is, in fact, my tribe of Retirement Rebels.

Sincere thanks to the We Make Stuff Happen Team in Vancouver, Canada, for creating and hosting my website and looking after my domain names.

Huge thanks go to The ASK Method Company for helping me create two strategic quizzes and for coaching me to navigate the digital marketing world. I would like to commend founder Ryan Levesque, marketing experts Peter Li and Blake Stepan, and most especially my personal coach, Kurt Wuerfele, for his firm yet generous direction.

I'm thankful to Nigel Sutherland, one of the UK's foremost cartoonists, for the eight cartoon illustrations for each of the chapters of this book.

I'm most grateful to Judy O'Beirn and her team at Hasmark Publishing International, including Anne Karklins, Amit Dey, Harshita Sharma, Jenn Gibson, Jenna Ventura, Niki Rowland, and Allison Burney for helping in transforming my manuscript into a published book.

Last but not least, a huge thank you in advance to my clients, my followers, my tribe of Retirement Rebels, and to the entire baby boomer generation, whose destiny has been to change the world for the better.

ABOUT THE AUTHOR

GEORGE JERJIAN is a mindset mentor, author, and speaker who retired after being given just six months to live by his doctor. Thankfully, the diagnosis was wrong and as soon as he could, he "unretired" and set to work, helping his tribe of baby boomers do the same.

George has a business degree from Bradford University in England and a master's degree in journalism from New York University. He has been in business for over 40 years, working as a Chartered Marketer, a partner in US commercial real estate, and a financial adviser. He has authored 10 books, is an Emmy award-winning producer, a Distinguished Toastmaster, and founder of Retirement Rebellion.

OTHER BOOKS BY GEORGE JERJIAN

- Seven Ages; Personal Financial Planning (1997)
- The Battle of the Portals (1999)
- Ecosystem: Living the 12 Principles of e-Business (2001)
- Xerox Firestorm 2001
- The Truth Will Set Us Free: Armenians and Turks Reconciled (2003)
- Sarkis Izmirlian: A Biography (2008)
- Seeking God: A Pilgrimage in the Holy Land (2013)
- Arabkir (2014)
- Daylight After a Century (2015)
- Spirit of Gratitude: Crises are Opportunities (2018)

Made in the USA
Las Vegas, NV
03 March 2023